Margaret,

Stephen says this is the
best book ever!

Best,
Eve Mayer Orsburn
@LinkedInQueen

What Executives say about EVE MAYER ORSBURN'S

Social Media for the CEO

*The Why and ROI of Social Media
for the CEO of Today and Tomorrow*

"The social web provides a new way of listening to and engaging with consumers. Think about the opportunities the web provides for listening companies. Eve Mayer Orsburn's book provides rich case studies from respected brands. The insight and sage advice are there for the taking."

- Mary Henige, *APR/Director of Social Media &
Digital Communications, General Motors Company*

"This is a no-nonsense guide with real-world examples as to how a strategic approach to social media can help any CEO improve the top and bottom lines. The principles of Eve's "Social Media Equation" detailed in the book can be applied to all organizations, no matter what type or size."

- Kent Huffman, *Chief Marketing Officer, BearCom Wireless
Co-Publisher of Social Media Marketing Magazine*

"Learning a new 'language' while challenging is very rewarding. Communicating in the language your employees and colleagues do shows you are a 'with-it' leader. Social networking is the language of this generation and Eve has crafted the instruction manual to teach you the skills necessary to leverage the power of it to build your business and team."

- TJ Schier, *President, S.M.A.R.T. Restaurant Group*

"If you want to learn about social media and how to leverage your business then you need to read this book and more importantly read it and apply what you have read to your business. Eve Mayer Orsburn has harnessed more knowledge than most people will ever know about social media and shares it in this book in an entertaining, inspiring and easy to apply format that makes it hard to put down. You will learn more from reading it than taking hours of classes."

- Patty Farmer, *Founder/CEO, Biz Link Global Owner, HPM Dallas Business Networking, Discounts & Benefits*

"In her book, *Social Media for the CEO*, Eve Orsburn has explained the new world of social media in such a way that its intimidation is replaced with obvious opportunity. Through her ability to make what appears complex, simple and strategic, it becomes easy to capitalize on what is truly a revolution in the way people communicate, interact and make decisions. It is a must read for anyone serious about moving their company forward into the world of online media."

- John D. Marvin, *President, Texas State Optical*

"In the financial industry there are countless regulations that make social media a scary endeavor, but this book, *Social Media for the CEO*, explains why an organization must engage in social media now and that there are ways to do this within the confines of every industry. Even a high-end brand steeped in years of tradition should be exploring this brave new world of social media for its ability to leverage communication in a more powerful way than ever before."

- Julia N. Danklef, *Director, Bernstein Global Wealth Management*

"Social media represents a fundamental shift in the way businesses interact with their customers. This book breaks through the hype that surrounds the subject and offers clear advise on how organisations can embrace this new communications channel. It uncovers how to create a compelling investment case and nurture a loyal customer base."

- Ivan Gunatilleke, *COO, Cable & Wireless Worldwide*

"Recognizing that social media is today's communication connection to a new and younger market, the Museum moved quickly to acquire the outside talent we needed to catch the trend. What a great decision for us! We are currently one of the most followed Museums in America on Twitter. Other institutions are contacting us for advice. Thousands of people who would otherwise never have heard of us are now our friends and supporters."

- Wanda R. Brice, *CEO, The Women's Museum*

"I completely overhauled my social media approach and campaign based on Eve's concepts and recommendations. The response has been unbelievable! We have sky rocketed to the number one tweeted hotel in Fort Worth, Texas all within 90 days. When it comes to market domination, Eve is the Queen."

- Paul Chaston, *Director of Sales and Marketing, Sheraton Fort Worth Hotel and Spa*

"Eve really gets the social media phenomenon. I really enjoy her communication style. This book, *Social Media for the CEO*, is fun and provides needed knowledge, an unusual combination."

- David Boyett, *CEO/Owner of Boyett Management Services Group Chair, Vistage International*

"I've learned through personal business experience that in the 21st Century, even if you have an incredibly remarkable product or service, you cannot dominate an industry without a solid platform in social media. Eve's book, *Social Media for the CEO*, is THE "go-to" guide in understanding and creating a cohesive plan of social media action for your brand."

— Fleetwood Hicks, *President, Villy Customs*

"Eve's straightforward approach of making businesses understand the value and necessity of social media comes through loud and clear with this book. So many people still discount social media as a tool for college kids and movie stars, but being able to see the ROI through case studies should open their eyes. Her company, Social Media Delivered, launched my hotel into the social media mainstream and we could not have done it without them."

— Kimberly Hutcherson, *President,*
Hospitality Sales & Marketing Association International DFW
Director of Sales, Hampton Inn Dallas/Irving-Las Colinas, Texas

Emerging Media Press

For ordering information, special discounts for bulk purchases or to book the author as a speaker, please visit www.SocialMediafortheCEO.com or call +1 469.248.0616.

Edited by Rusty Fischer
Proofread by Andi Reis
Book Cover and Layout Design by Jamie Nanquil

Case Study research, writing, and proofreading assistance by Amanda Montgomery, Amelia Clark, Angelo Fernandez-Spadaro, Mary B. Adams, Laura Hale, Katy Mendelsohn, Ruth Ferguson and Shilpa Nicodemus

FIRST EDITION

Library of Congress Cataloging-in-Publication data is available upon request.

ISBN 978-0-615-39306-3

2010934217

Social Media for the CEO

*The Why and ROI of Social Media
for the CEO of Today and Tomorrow*

EVE MAYER ORSBURN

Emerging Media Press

This book is dedicated to my family

Guy & Regina Mayer, my parents, who started it

Rob Orsburn, my husband, who supported it

Mia Mayer Orsburn, my daughter, who makes it all worth it

This book would not have been possible or made sense without my online connections and friends. Thank you:

@162030251 @18002228477 @_____1 @__haus @__mesothelioma_ @__wahpapa @_7th_Chakra @_alexyr_ @_Allejandro_ @_AllyssaMarie_ @_AnilThakur @_Archie
@_artemiy @_AutomaticGeek @_ayudame @_BOWILD @_BTE @_chimes_ @_ClareOliver_ @_cloudgirl @_cric_ @_darlene_davis @_davidhenry_ @_DebbieRussell
@_e_bomb @_EarnExtraMoney @_EricLundberg_ @_Fast_ @_FNDS3000 @_GeorgeL @_iChRiS_ @_jul @_justthinking @_landscaping @_lauramckay_ @_M_A_C
@_MakeQuickMoney @_McLaughlin @_MeioAmbiente_ @_Olga_ @_palomilla @_pathmaker @_Poschi_ @_praedo_ @_QFI_ @_Redux @_RickRage_ @_SEM
@_seo_consulting @_Sheila_ @_ShoTyme_ @_Signalfire_ @_so_so_ @_socialeyes @_spell @_thetwitguy @_toinfinity @_Umwelt @_webguru @_Why_Ask @_wigs
@_Woman_health @_WordGirl @007Diva @007joectms @007LouiseOB @007phantom @01cypark @0bivan @0boy @0clickmylit @0Frank @0thevalentines0 @0utKast
@1001blogs @1001topwords @100acres @100days2victory @100KAMonth @100kMLM @100x100net @100Zeros @1031ExchangeNOW @104Tips @1055webdesign @1080Group
@108antiaging @10training @10yearsofbb @1154LillKC @11health9 @11kx @11taste24 @123_Refills @123movie @123peopleNL @123sexy_undies @123socialmedia @123teens
@123top10 @1248webdesign @1337studios @1337windows @13rittny3 @1400words @140College @140LoveBird @140twitstreet @1495bk @15pts @173Sud @1800GETLENS
@1800petinsure @1800pools @1800RUNAWAY @18884PageRocket @1975jmr @19SIXTY5 @1aurence @1BizLeader @1bluemarz @1BreakingNews @1brownmoUse
@1Businessman @1BYBY @1CASTentertain @1CASTfinance @1CASTtech @1ChessKing @1chicgeek @1Chingishan @1DanFeildman @1datarecovery @1FreedomFeed
@1Green1Blue @1highlife @1HoustonNews @1jameshunter @1jasim @1LosAngelesNews @1lovely_friend @1LX @1makemoney1 @1MCB1 @1miaan @1MILLIONBBMUSER
@1mindone @1MonthFacelift @1mwilson @1NBUSINESS @1New_Life @1ok @1onlinestore @1opportunity @1PhillyNews @1picstory @1rene @1robward @1sassy_chick
@1scottcarson @1securityguru @1Sky @1SocialMrkting @1st_Commentary @1stblogger @1stdjs @1stDUBLI @1stPositionMktg @1TD @1to1coach @1txsage1957
@1webworld @1wisechick @2_Pears @2000thor @2010_APRIL @2010_FEBRUAR @2010_JANUAR @2010_JANUARY @2010_Vision @2010paradise @2010valentine
@2012DeathWatch @2012files @2012revealed @2015wpfg @20Community @20somethingca @214Fresh @21CenturyDental @21cwr @21inc @21stlaur @22Rockwell
@23rmorandantejr @247hotinfo @247legaladvice @247tweet @2500group @256Mbps @2574Design @25dl @25weightloss @26DotTwo @29DayFacelift @2add @2addme
@2ADu @2BidOnAWish @2big4mybuttons @2BitViews @2charity @2commonsense @2cre8 @2Debbie @2don @2DreamIt @2e2UK @2guyslawnmower @2helppeople
@2hospitality @2jsmarketing @2LittleShihTzus @2Marra @2mfox @2moroDocs @2morrowknight @2mysticmountain @2NeverWorkAgain @2osto @2PromoteU
@2rise @2savelives @2SELLHOMES @2sleepbetter @2StayAtHomeMom @2tammytodd @2thespot @2tweetwitheric @2tweetyou @2urfuture @2win1big @3_shera
@3_wise_men @301STUDIOS @30DayFacelift @30dayturnaround @30wastedyears @312info @31DayFacelift @321deins @33_smile @333AutismNews @333AutismNews3
@360executive @360social @360sxswi @360VideoMapping @360WebEx @360wellnessguy @36Terabytes @380Dentist @3amor @3dayme @3days_in_london
@3dgamestudio @3dimensionalife @3DInternet @3dMildred @3dogmarketing @3dpoker @3DPorn1 @3elva57 @3fifty7music @3FOUR1 @3frogs @3GLebenskonzept
@3iInfotech @3rdcorner @3rdpartyblog @3v3rytingiswack @3viewHD @3WDesign @3WDesignMedia @4_Squared @411_HomeDecor @411bloggingguide @440tv
@451Heat @4BetWithAir @4BW @4byoung @4CloseYOURDeal @4Compression @4entrepreneur @4giv @4JustUsWW @4kaylin @4linkedlearning @4loveofcoffee
@4psmarketing @4ralph @4S @4SEMktg @4sqday @4theloveofmike @4tsubasa @4usaul @4wardfinancial @500Ksystem @506properties @509Beaderynews
@50bookchallenge @52Nine @52weekfootball @59minlearning @5bliss @5eo @5FiguresAMonth @5FtHighMktgGuy @5Great @5Ideas @5JKL @5le @5pointedstar
@5tevenw @5thStreetPizza @600conf @60plusfriends @614NewMedia @617patrick @61surebet @62Labs @630info @666mkt1 @68bashirum68 @6aliens @6figs4u
@6FiguresForLife @700t @714dragon @720Strategies @73K @74thnpark @7573Marketing @76sixer @777stocks @78EET @7degreescom @7figures @7HUNNIT
@7KeysToDeductIt @7LD @7NewsQLD @7thscreen @7wishes @847info @888jeffcline @888starmedia @88thegreat @8BroadSt @8dhd @8ightyNine @8packabs
@8thandWalton @8VisionsofHope @90sMillionaire @911worldinfo @95millionaires @99_design @9INCHmarketing @9swords @9xhot @A_Aviles @A_Big_Discount
@a_estrategico @a_greenwood @A_Lan @a_shoobs @a_smart_union @A1business4u @A1dogtraining @A1SURFus @a2zShoes @A3aanxl @aaambler @AAAResumes
@aabcdewi @Aadii_ @AAirwaves @aajain @aakarpost @AaltoSpreadson @aamandabieber @Aan_Afdi @AandASocialMktg @aanetwork @AAOdds @aarfmike
@aargenz1 @aaronabber @aaronadamson @AaronBiddar @aarond22 @aaronhackett @AaronHoos @AaronInTexas @AaronMSanchez @AaronParsons @aaronpost
@aaronrayo @aarrona @AAshmam @aatif_ahmed05 @AB_Thomas @abaci1790 @Abadi_Access @abaigorriaz @AbaloneHome @Abazy901 @abbelt @Abbey22239
@Abbott2010 @abbybrown24 @abbylocke @abbyse @abbytaylor14 @abdulkarim @ABDWellness @abeahanfnp @abeles @abellastudios @Abendkleider @AberOnline
@ABetterAnswer @ABetterResume @abfo @abfromz @abfsra @AbhayPatil @abhijitdas1982 @abhishek_gupta @abie_maria @abigailming @abirb123 @abjay @abokroslife
@aboutbanks @aboutdietnews @AboutGameCheats @aboutpolitics @abovegame @abovethelevel @AboveTheStatic @ABradbury @abrahamharrison @abroaderview
@abrownplante @abrudtkuhl @abs4ever @absalam2 @absiemorrison @absolit @absolutamber @Absolutely_Abby @AbsolutelyJay @AbsolutelyPR @absolutpac @abssd
@AbsurdistTaxi @AbtGratitude @Abundance__ @abundance4you @AbundanceBound @AbundanceExpo @abundantwater @AcademicDemon @AcademicHelp @AcademicJobs
@AcadianaEats @Acaiultimate @acastrillon @acatalanello @access_basics @access_geeks @accessbarbados @accesssonora @ACCHBdotCOM @AccomandTravel
@Accommotel @AccordionGuy @AccountancyGuru @accountingjobz @AccountPrepaid @AccountSitter @accrete @Acctg411 @AcctMgrJessica @AccuGuy @AccurateData
@AccurateMailInc @acdcfan3 @AceFreeman52387 @Aceinternet @acelfl @Acenamers @Acentuate @acezadams @Ach1mO @AChelsian @achievereffect @AchimBurgardt
@AchimMuellers @acholitek @Achordus @achristiansen @ACI_C5marketing @acid89 @acmcleaning @acmontgomery @acmsomyos @acndave @acnehelphq @acneinfos
@acoverthypnosis @ACPLAN @ACPundit @acquisio @AcrossTheDivide @actioevent @actionchick @actionczar @ActionGirlAPC @ActionManage @ActionREI
@actionScript3 @actionwealth @Activ8business @ActiveEdgeTeam @ActivegameZ @ActiveIngreds @activeinterview @activenetwork @ActiveRain @activesearcher
@ActOfficial @actonyourcallin @ActorAshley @actplatinum @acuam @acutler @acydlord @ad_syner @ADA_KINGS @ADAH90068957 @adalys08 @Adam_Kraker
@adam_mega @adam_smith233 @Adam_TrackDaddy @adam_whitaker @AdamAdame @adamaltman @adamandstevesto @adamboyden @adamcadell @AdamChapnick
@adamcohen @adamfrench34 @AdamHoldenBache @AdamLeeBowers @adamlisk1 @adamlucas25 @adamostrow @adamreiter @AdamRock @adamsangster @adamsconsulting
@adamsherk @AdamSpiel @adamterw @adamwrichard @adaptick @AdastraPR @adbean_net @adbert @Add1000Follower @Adda_White @Addicted_Gamers @addictedtwit
@addisonpointe @Addisson @additionsstyle @AddMeOnLinkedin @addoway @Ade1965 @Adeah @AdeccoThailand @adelamathiwe @AdelNews @adevries @adformatie
@ADHDcure @adhywu973 @Adi_Avi @adiletchaim @adindustryvoice @adisaan @adit82a @adityabhatt @AdJuice @adleer22 @adlt_lifestyle @Admance @AdManJosephG
@admarketpros @AdmitOneTix @admixsocial @adnzafar @AdogyNetwork @adolforosado @AdoptAPett @adoptedbabies @adoptingapet @AdrenalynnINK @adri72 @adriaanrainso
@AdrianaArvizo @adrianalove @adrianchira @AdrianeHigdon @adrianfleischer @AdrianLee @AdrianMelrose @AdrianneMachina @adriansoare @adriansutanto @adrianswinscoe
@adrielhampton @adrienneaudrey @AdrienneCorn @AdrienneLJ @AdrienneRehm @adriereinders @AdriJ @Adrita1 @AdRockia @ads2txt @adsmove @adsoftheworld
@adstand @adtrend @aDuchan @ADufriesVSS @adultorphan @AdvAmerica @AdvantageTaxRes @adventuregirl @AdventureLive @AdventurePass @adventurepeople
@AdvertisersNet @Advertising_UK @AdvertisingInfo @AdvertisingLaw @AdvertisingNerd @AdvertisingPR @AdvertisingSMS @advertlive @AdviceScene @advicesisters @advick
@Advisor_Marcus @AdweekDotCom @adwrighty @AdzZoo_SEO2010 @adzzoocrew @AdzZooReps @AECarter @AEKeleher6 @aellislegal @aemikel @aemmajg
@aeohn @AeroAngels @AerobicsOnline @Aerocles @AeroFade @aerospacejob1 @aetherstrike @afalk @AFasterPC @aff_cash @Affaircare @affiliantes @affiliate_buddy
@affiliateaces @affiliatearmada @affiliatecircle @AffiliateDesk00 @affiliatefaith @AffiliateFlower @AffiliateNews4u @AffiliatePro64 @affiliateprobiz @affiliates2
@AffiliateStar12 @affiliatetank @AffiliateTeam @affiliatetoday @AffiloScott @AffiniaChicago @AffirmationBlog @AffirmYourLife @AffluenceNow @Affnet @affsum
@afftraction @afieryphoenix @AfifaMasood @afiliatemarket @AFlirtYourself @afmasudivre @AFollowerForYou @afritainment @AfroditeLaceWig @AfroMarketing
@AFrugalFriend @aftercurfew @afterdoorportal @afterschool4all @AftrHrsAutoGlas @AFutureWithout @afvanwingerden @Agabhumi @AGAconnection @Agape_Church
@agardina @agboise @ageasoft @agebackwards @AgelessSecret @agenceb2b @AgencyBabylon @AgendaVoiceover @agentcesd @AgentDeepak @AgentJester @AgentNews
@Agentopolis @agentsmiller @AgentsOnline @agentspayforwrd @agentwealthproj @AgeoLopez @agguley @aghreni @agideon @Agile_Cat @agiledudes @AgilePoint
@agiletechnosys @agooddaughter @agoodeye @agoramedia @agquillinan @AgribizNews @agromaximum @agsocialmedia @aguitarguy95 @agunn @agus_setiyawan
@agusbilly @agusnadhi @ahall3649 @ahamany @aHappinessCoach @AHartFly @ahaval @ahblackledge @AHCSolutions @aheart4god @aheartforgod @aheneghana
@ahhhgolf @AhhPhotography @AHLDickherber @ahmad_m_salem @ahmad94 @ahmansoor @AhomeZ @ahopton70 @AHPediatrics @Ahrnertyg @ahsanmedia @AiAbdullah
@Aianna95 @aidkits @aiesya69 @aigostyle @aihui @aikomita @AileenAvikova @AileenFlicki @AIM4Marketing @aimeecheek @aimeepilz @AimeeSilly @Aimegsinha
@AIMIAqld @AIMTherapy @ainebelton @air_condition @air_cooling @air_cut @air1radio @AiraBongco @Airbrush_Makeup @Aireslibre @AirGorilla @airspersona
@AIRSTraining @airwalk_online @AishaGlen @AishahC_Designs @aishaofpr @AisleShops @aivalis @Aiye @aj_affiliate @aj_wood @AJ2D @ajanijackson @AjayJacobsen
@AJdigitalFocus @ajhalls2 @Ajidon @AjinkyaForYou @ajjoseph @ajkasza @ajuliano @ajwebmarketing @ajwilcox @ajwire @aka_mike @AkakAtak @akalfa @akalous
@akanaliga @AkankshaGoel @akearns @AkgeeSports @akhaleque @akikojes @akintibubo @akinyelestephen @AkiraMas @akleinschmidt @akmanda @akoneill
@AkosFintor @AKpicks @akquisefachfrau @AkramBiz @AKREMORFIN @akromanelli @akrongarber @AkronOhioHomes @aktiff08 @AktivDigital @akuinginsukses
@akula33 @Al3XIII @al999 @Alabye_com @alagirir @Alain_Lemay69 @AlaisterLow @AlAltan @alan_sharland @alan_sills @AlanaKarran @alanbobet @alanbr82
@AlaneAnderson @alange710 @alangent5000 @AlanGeorgeBrook @alanhaft @alanjenkin @alanjingram @alankerrigan @AlanLCaldwell @AlanLopuszynski @AlanMcGeeSay
@AlanRae @AlanRainey @AlanSee @alanunderkofler @alanwhite101 @alanxing @alapplegate @alasandy @AlaskaArtist @alaskahwybb @AlaskaMoose @AlaskaSpeaks
@ALauderdale @alawine @AlbemarlePlant @albertagurl1 @albertopayo @AlboNumismatico @AlchemyLab @alchimagica @AlcidesCF @AlcoheimersNO @AlcottHRGroup
@ALD85 @AldaRRissel @ALDO1958 @aldsaur @alduque @aldyboy_03 @alead @aleandrade @alecberg @alecorreo @alecsandruan @alejarami2096 @AleksAtanasov
@aleksnrg @alemaksymon @alenhoff @Aleska777 @AlessandraCo @AlethaMcManama @AleWriter @Alex_185 @alex_90 @Alex_Dorian @Alex_Ionescu
@Alex_Joungblood @alex_knorr @alex_marketer @alex_ping @Alex_Tomm @Alex14112412 @alexa86ab @AlexaAdrian @alexabi @alexaesthetics @alexanderamanda
@alexanderbrom @Alexandermay @Alexandra_lo69 @Alexandra_Mary @AlexandraFish @AlexandraRyan @AlexandreBonin @AlexAndrei @alexandreruoso @alexandriaFry
@alexandrocastro @alexasamuels @alexasdad @alexbacks @AlexBlom @alexbobadilla @alexdallison @alexdc @AlexDogy @alexdrogeanu @alexgarcia @AlexGrech
@Alexhamil @alexiaanastasio @alexica73 @alexico_swim @alexingloire @AlexinHouston @AlexisCeule @alexisvandam @AlexKaris @AlexLelodLarrea @AlexLimInc
@alexlockwood @Alexluvmusic @alexmatatula @alexnester @AlexPapaCom @alexpuig @AlexResolutions @AlexSchleber @AlexShapiroWR @AlexSimpsonLOVE @alexsol
@alextoul @AlFerretti @alfina87 @alfmarcussen @alfonsoromans @AlfredoSMS @algoRhythmLabs @alhanzal @Ali_Dee @Ali_Kurt @aliayvaz @alibabaoglan @alicam
@Alice200806 @aliceheiman @alicemurphie @AliceTChan @alicia_pierce @aliciacastillo @Aliciadawn2008 @aliciafalcone @aliciamarie112 @aliciamejia @AliciaSanera
@aliciaslander @aliciaXziel @alidark3000 @Alienbeing @ALIENDIMENSIONS @alienguide @AlignProsperity @AlignYourEnergy @alihooper @aliinspired @AlikBarsegian
@AlilSunshine4U @AliMaynard @Alin_S @AlinaAlison @alinekefr @AlineLii @alingham @alinnear1 @AlinsSonMullins @AlioGenetics @AlionaKJewelry @alisaa99
@alisfoster @AlishaNorris @AlishaTV @AlisonBLowndes @AlisonDoyle @alisondrake @AlisonHeld @alisonjns @alisonlaw @alisonrbcm @Alisoranger @AlisPeraza
@AlissaFereday @alissasadler @AliveNewZealand @AlkalineBuzz @AlkalineH2O @alkhemst @alkomy @All_A_Baut_HCM @all_aboard_surf @all4freebies @AllAboutHer
@allaboutpaws @allabouturskin @AllAbtChristmas @AllAbtDogs @AllAbtFamily @AllAbtLove @AllaBurda @AllanBBeaton @AllanCrawford @allancurtis @allanp73

@allanpearlman @allanschoenberg @allantowns @allanwaldron @allcapetown @allcaughtup @AllDallas @Allen_Tx @allenbostrom @AllenCordrey @allenmireles
@allenmowery @AllenonBlackSea @AllenRhoadarmer @AllenVoivod @AllenWebstar @Allerent @allflo @allialexander @allianceintl @Alliebrwneyez @alliemiami
@alliey_marie @AllInOneOutlet @allison_w @allisoncrawfo21 @AllIThatIs @Allman_C_ @allneedo @ALLNEWSN @allonsdanser @allowinglife @AllSheriffSales
@AllStagesMktg @AllTalent @AllTechTronics @AllTexanMusic @AllThingsGwen @alltopquotes @AllYap @AllYapp @allygill @AllysePadden @allysimone @allysonmorgan
@AllysonMorris @AllysonRKring @AlmaLasers @AlmaNova @AlmineSabia @AlmineWijsheid @almond_beauty @almondpeak @almostfearless @ALNEVCorp
@AloeAloe2u @aloebiz4u @AloeTropical @AloftDallas @AlohaArleen @alokc @alokonlinejob99 @aloktiwari @alom_205 @alpa83 @AlpacaFarmgirl @AlPeggy
@alpenwest @Alpha_Computer @alphaedefense @alphaengineer2 @alphahelicopter @Alphalist @AlphaMares @AlphaPie @alphatweet2 @Alprimocanto @alrai
@alrassociation @ALRCoach @alsagora @alt164 @Altaide_JF @Altec_Angel @AltEnergyWebPar @AlternativeHeat @AlternativeNRG @althea_martin @AltMedicineBlog
@altmktg @Altpap @altt1 @alucididea @alunrichards @alvaresotero @AlvesFilipe @alvinbrown @alvincbeyer @AlvinSchmitt @alvinycheung @alwayscatholic
@alwaysfinance @AlWoods @AlxRodz @alyandrea @alysdrake @alyssaavant @alyssagregory @alyssonneves @alywalansky @AlzayCalhoun @amacowboys451 @amahouston
@amalari @Amanda_Upspring @Amanda_vdGulik @Amanda_Warr @amandaaviles1 @amandachapel @AmandaDCMS @amandahawk @amandakathryn @amandakrill
@AmandaMarieBlog @AmandaMCarter @amandasback @AmandaVega @amandertising @AMAnet @amankumra @amapoda @amarc_afxisi @amarkule @amartintx @amasv
@AmayaPapayasmom @amazedlive @AmazinglyAmara @amazinglyblog @AmazingPictures @amazingreality @amazingvidtours @amazonamit @AmazonSecret @Ambal
@ambassador0112 @amber_design @amber01 @Amber69nf @AmberCadabra @AmberDeVille @amberpresley @amberr_2014 @AmberReiki @Ambitiouspeople
@AmCapitalfundng @AMCForg @AmConsUnified @ameliachen @AmeliaEChampion @Ameliahomes @ameliawoods @AmericaCalling @AmericanEnt @Americanext
@AmericanIssues @AmericanLaser @AmericanMktg @AmericanWomannn @AmericasAgenda @americaspress @amesinora @amforever @amfunderburk1 @amfurie
@amgenove @amhartnett268 @AmHealthBeauty @ami_zhasayhu @Ami3251 @AmiAhuja @amiedigital @amihealthsvs @Amin1uk @aminoff @amirbq @amirk25
@amitanigam @amitcpatel @amitgautam @amitibudhrani @amitm68 @amjadhkhan @AMLassociates @AMm2studios @ammore @ammuappoze @amoils @AMORC11
@amorfar @Amorous_VI @amosays @amous @ampc @Amped4News @Ampiphy @ampli2de @AMPTAgency @amraxx @amrcon @amsandrew1 @amsonline @AmSpirit
@amtower @AmUNESCO @amusingsexfacts @AMVdudes @amwatmovers @amyanderson01 @AmyatMovingOn @amybeer @amygiambruno @Amygirl2006 @amyhammond
@amyhasslen @AmyJantzer @AmyKinnaird @amykr @amylambright @AmyLinderman @AmyLynnAndrews @AmyMSimon @amyoutloud @AmyP00h @amys_bus_ticket
@amysmlmfortune @AmyStark @AmyStarrAllen @AmyVernon @AmyWSYX6 @AmyyMack @amzhealthcare @An1malCrazy @AnaCarterOnline @AnacondaWOW
@anadeau @AnaGirl22 @anaknyte @AnaliFirst @AnaLoback @AnaLuciaNovak @Analytics_USA @analytixman @anamarquez1 @Anan_Lashin @anandaleeke @AnaNogales
@AnaRC @AnasaziStories @anbazhagan @anccricket @anchalsingh @anchorwomen @andaruandru @AndBreak @anddjournal @andgenth @andicurry @andiepetoskey
@andikadewan @andilinks @andimarlon @AndMoreComm @Andrea_Wolo @andreabeadle @andreacarless @andreacook @AndreaDeaPachec @AndreaHoxie
@AndreaJordanuk @AndreaMeyer @andreamoffat @AndreaNowack @andreas_derksen @AndreaSatter @AndreasLeo @andreastenberg @andreaswpv @andreatarrant
@AndreaVahl @AndreBiester @AndredeBeer @AndreiCurelaru @AndreInfobase @andreitoup @Andreiuk @Andres_Luna @AndresD @andreseloynava @AndresFabris
@andressilvaa @Andrew_Boyd @Andrew_Johnson @andrew_murray @Andrew_Skelly @andrew9963 @AndrewBates @andrewbrenner @andrewcbrooks @AndrewCiccone
@andrewdaum @andrewfoote @andrewhesselden @andrewjlingley @andrewkeir @AndrewKuhn @AndrewLedford @Andrewlock @AndrewOpala @andrewrondeau
@andrews1tweet @andrewspoeth @AndriaStanley @AndroidPower @Andromeda95 @AndrosCreations @Andy_Burton @andy_dmxpert @andy_fuller @andy_proper
@Andy_Stanczyk @andycarroll @andycooktellem @andyheadworth @andyhughes @AndyInNaples @andylloydgordon @andymac71 @Andymantweet @AndyMichaels121
@andymurd @andyraj @AndyShaw67 @AndyWinchell @anechan @AnemosNaftilos @anepiphany @anerushprnews @anesiderman @anestatehunter @anetah @anewbook
@Anewulivin @Angarastones @angarie @Angel_Oliverio @angel_voices @Angel4tweet @angela_nelson @Angela_Paige @angelabosscher @AngelaCrocker @angelakokorudz
@AngelaLapre @angelambrown @angelarden @Angelatida @AngelaWills @angelic_fez @Angelina54 @AngelinaMunaret @AngellaRaisian @angellr @angeloantoni
@AngeloHall @angelovidiri @angelscassidy @angelscreus @AngelsDen @AngelsKnocking @Angelsoft @AngelWardriver @Angesilva_ @Angie_Perez @Angieatcougar
@angiechaplin @AngieElenis @angiefit4040 @angiepeady @AngieStrader @AngieSwartz @AnglumGroup @angpaige_ @angrywhitedude @angshu_tnmg4u
@Angus__McDonald @angusfraserDXB @anicho @AniChristy @AnideArt @anikabelle @anikogiampietro @AnikoLecoultre @AnilSalick @animal @AnimalHolistic
@anir27 @AnishKumarSingh @aniskhan1 @anison_spirits @AnissaW08 @anissiddiqi @AnitaDFiouris @anitafiander @anitaideas @AnitaMatys @AnitaMHicks @anitasantiago
@AnjaHoffmann @Anjawerkt @anjum121 @ankiep @ankitmendapara @ankurdinesh @ankush225 @AnkushKohli @Ann_imal @ann731735 @anna_dean @anna_rich
@annabellalamp @AnnaJ31 @annalaurabrown @Annalilie @annalisabluhm @AnnaXYates @AnnaZ @AnnBotham @annbrine @AnnCollins @annconvery23 @anndouglas
@anne_bain @AnneDGallaher @AnneEgros @AnneGogh @anneharpen @annejoyce @AnneliesVro @AnnelizeFaul @AnnemarieCross @annemariemilton @annemiejanssens
@Annemieke_C @AnneMSwinehart @annesoul @anneterbraak @AnnetteatAlstin @Anngelica @annharrell @annholman @Annie_Fox @AnnieArmen @anniebananie76
@annielustig @AnniesBlogs @AnniesParadise @AnnieStrack @annievang @annika @annikaek @Annita_Lee @annitot @AnnLuo1998 @annmariehanlon @annmarieWineset
@annmartinphotog @AnnMcCaughan @AnnoyedByU @annpadgett @AnnRabson @annschilling @AnnualMusicWeek @Anny4000 @anonymous1mill @anonymousjonez
@Anorocagency @Ansaco @anscahomes @Ansolu_20 @answermen @AntHeald @anthemedge @AnthillMagazine @anthishiten @Antho_tompenk @anthodges
@anthony_wilson @anthonyarrigali @AnthonyB1 @AnthonyBasich @AnthonyCrecco @anthonycurtis @AnthonyGemma @anthonygunning1 @AnthonyKershaw
@AnthonyMcMurray @anthonymcneil @AnthonyMoraPR @AnthonyNelson @anthonyonesto @anthonysanti @AnthonyWenham @Anthrodigital @Anti_Pollution
@antiagingnetwrk @antifoton @antoine_c @antoinepatricia @antoniocuauro @antonioechols @antoniogimeno @AntonioRestaur @AntonioTalent @antonius0 @antonroy
@AntonStetner @antonycw @antorio @Antoshka_Sk @antotea2 @Anubhavspeaks @AnuffSaidInc @anumber1air @Anunciato @anupamrajey @anupchowdhury
@anushaverma @anveso @AnvilPhilly @AnwarSafar @anxietyhelp4U @anyadowning @anybizsoft @anylondon @anyotosetiadi @AnythingAnthony @anywaytosave
@AOAweb @AOBA_TETSUO @AOD_Lois @aoljobs @AOLRadio @AomDAY @AP_THE_REBEL @apanafashion @apbyers @apegan @APejic @ApertureDaily
@apfelmonster_de @api_mashup @apinkerton @APInt @aplacetobark @APLINK @Aplus_net @APMike @ApogeeCampaigns @apombalivre @Apostlemarvin
@ApothecaryJeri @apparelgiant @AppAssure @AppetizersNOW @Appforthat_ @appitalism @AppJmp @appleifreak @AppleInvestor @applemacbookpro @AppQuotes
@approachmarket @appshouter @appsourus @ApptmtJournal @appz6 @AprilBraswell @aprilbroussard @aprilgregory @AprilPust @APrince15 @aPrioriDiamonds
@aprograms @AprStorm @AprylEhmann @AptsForRent @apurvarc @AQILITY @Aqua_Duke @aqua_spring @AquaBlueWeb @AquaDesignGroup @aquariumconcept
@AquiferMedia @ArabObserver @aragoncalidad @aragornara @araujofabio @aravindbabuv @ARBetts @arbitainc @ArbiterGamble @arbonneteam @Arborplex_DFW
@Arcade140 @arcadedig @archarlieber @ArchHappyHour @archiijs @arctictrend @ArcyEm @ardakert @Arddrive @ardentisys @Area224 @arealestateplan @arelt
@arena84 @arenosf @arethabest @Arethusa_Biz @arewers @areyouworthit @arfoodbank @ArgentaArtwalk @argentbeauquest @argus27 @Argvineyardclub @ArianaStones
@ARich323 @aridoliveira @AriellaCalinPR @arifamca @Arigo_The_Movie @ArimaxPharma @aristotlebuzz @ArizonaFlooring @arkarthick @arketi @ARKit_Plus @Arleen14
@ArleneTaveroff @ArliissonxD @ArlingtonAlerts @armadillostudio @Armando_Holguin @armikoadm @armourcleaning @Arnab_Toronto @ArnaudJacobs @arnimadesign
@Arno_muc @ArnoldBeekes @ArnoldMLM @arnoldseoung @ArnoldsTeam @arnonbu4 @arnonbu7 @ArnoudMeijering @AROMANDINA @arora_sunil @arounme
@ARParty @ARStateParks @Art_Tee @ArtArgenio @artbythelake @artclubcaucasus @ArtechRoofing @ArtfromHeart @ArtGibbs @arthooker @ArthurAndSandye
@ArthurB1955 @arthurbonora @arthurcooper @ArthurCVanWyk @arthurra @ArthurTubman @ArticleBackLink @Articlemark44 @articlemarket00 @ArticleReleases
@ArticleSalad @ArticlesEngine @ArticlesFYI @ArticleSlash @articlr @Articoz @Articularnos @Artificialmktg @Artikelprofi @artimpress @artistberrada @artistico
@ArtJonak @artmonastery @artoflicensing @ArtOfOnline @ArtOfTweeting @artofwarMMA @artontile @Artook @artpainchaud @artretreats @ArtsCultureDFW @ArtseyC
@artshirtdesign @ArtTileMosaics @artuntravel @arturocanez @arturoperalta1 @artuvek @artworkwebsite @ArtyClub @ArubaAwaits @arugbylife @ArumugamPitchai
@arun4 @arunpattnaik @aruomiram @arvadayates @ArveeRobinson @Arvil_Lavigne @arysyahrial @arzzcom @AsAnuttara @asbestost @ASCCareerOffice @aschottmuller
@asesita @asgoodandbetter @ashankumar @ashantifoods @asheville_nc @AshevilleFM @AshevilleHair @AshleeKeating @ashleekeep @ashleighBot @ashley_greer
@ashley_wright @ashley0810 @AshleyAffeldt @ashleyapt @ashleydstanley @AshleyJJohnson @AshleyNetwork @AshleyS116 @AshleyTCaldwell @ashlijewelers @AshMcdowel
@ASHOK77 @AshOz @ashrodriguez22 @AshtonKutcherFC @Ashvin76 @ashwinsanghi @Ashymon @Asiablues @AsiaCams @asiaimages @AsianArtStore @AsianRamblings
@AsianStarGirl @asiawholesale @ask_larry @ask_mama @ask4ferguson @AskAaronLee @AskAboutTravel @AskAlicia @askarnett @AskAShopaholic @askbick
@askbillmitchell @askbuyusu @AskChrisJensen @AskCRMA @AskDanThePRMan @Askdavidchalk @AskDrGeorge @AskDrRoss @askgeorgeyeocom @askjacki
@askJayson @askjeffpaul @AskJerzijoe @askkencheung @AskKim @asklarry @asklarrynow @AskNannette @askrizzo @askrocco @asksail @AskShah @AskThatGuy
@AskTheParents @askthewoman @AskTimWade @AskVic @askvincentfl @AskYourCoachSam @aslesinski @asmashah @aSmoothieQueen @aspelbernd @aspenbill
@AspireShawn @aspoerri @Asriadi @AssaraLaser @Asselt @assetplanners @assistanttothe1 @AssistDiscovery @AssistTV @AssistWP @assuranceagency @AssurantCareers
@Assureweb @ASSURX @ast3v3nson @AST750 @astbnboy @astdOC @AStepAheadMedia @asterdata @AsteriskCreativ @astonish_alicia @astrack @AstroBabes
@Astrologer_raj @astronomymusic @astronomyrecord @AstroVigilante @asuntoasiat1 @ASusoeff @asvag @asweetp @atalieK @ATasteOfCandy @AtbattCares
@ATC_SocialMedia @ATECTraining @ateenoie @AthaAliTweets @athealthstore @AthenaComm @AthenaEast @AtHomeMarketing @aThumper @ATI_SDVOSB
@atimarketing @AtimKavi @atimothy79 @atkinsjennifer @ATL_ARTISTS @ATL_RealEstate @AtlantaMarketer @AtlantaRebath @atlantichigh @atltechgal @ATM_Machine
@atmillermusic @AtomicDC @atomicegg @atomicjackie @atoneplace @atravelagent @atrealtylux @AtriaEspanol @atriskyouth2010 @atroya @ATsLady @AttagirlsAttic
@ATTCottonBowl @AttendADHD @attheboutique1 @attJOBS @ATTMPress @attractionlaw42 @Attractorfactor @AttysCounsel @atukbest @AtYourLibrary
@Auction_Action @Auction_Gal @auctioncar @AuctionDirect @Auctionscam @AuctionTweeter @audidriven @audiencemachine @audioconexus @audiolympics
@audiomicro @AUDIOMUZIC @audiovideoblog @audreychernoff @audrog @aueueueboi @aufwandan @augieray @AugusteHS @augustfromhome @Auna_DenverMag
@AundrayC @AuntMyra @AuPairCare @AuPairDanmark @Aura_Adorer @AuraDentalVegas @AuraGroup @AuraSustain @aurelieponton @AurelioSisto @Auriella
@aurorabrown @aurorahealthpr @Aurume @Aussie_Geek @Aussie_Mossie @AussieAdrian @aussiechic @aussieissues @AussieLogos @AussieParawhore @AussieRocks
@aussietechhead @AussieTomTV @austars @austin_mls @Austin_Williams @AustinPike_I75 @austintweetups @AustinYC @australiamaxgxl @AustralianDeals
@AustrianEcon @austriannews @auswonderwoman @authenticsports @AuthorAlchemy @authorlaurasaba @AuthorNarea @AUTHORnRECOVERY @AutismTips @auto4insur
@autoaccessorywa @AutoBuilders @AutoDreamLife @autofollowback @autografik @automatedray @automedia @automotive_crm @Automotive_Jobs @AutomotiveLimo
@automotiveman @AutomotivMotion @AutopilotMLM @AutoRevo @autos_insurance @Autumnsell @auwebmanager @avaiIable @avantgardeinter @Avasiare @AventineHill
@Aventuramall @avenuegirl @Avenuehotel @AVerMediaUSA @aversitenteras @AveryCohen @AveryProducts @AveryTalk @aVg @avgconsumer @AvidCareerist
@avigenuine @AvilaNina @avilbeckford @avitalbez @avlcsfoundation @avmaster @AVMband @avocadogroove @AVONbyMindy @avondiva @avotaku_com @AVPpodcast
@AVPvolleyball @AVSRSA1 @avtopazar @AW_Systems @Awaiting2012 @AwakenDMarketR @awakeningaimee @AwakenToGod @awalshimaging @AwardEmployees
@awarenessmaster @AwareNetConnect @AWClub @awcyber @AWEbusiness @awesome_income @AwesomeInchLoss @AwesomeROAR @awienick @AwigaMedia
@awnawnow @AWOL @aworldforus @awscreative @axel2010a @Axioneering @AxisCentral @AxisNewMedia @axpz01 @AxsysTechGroup @ayamanalo @AyannaMurray
@AyBuey @AYCCarpet @ayegerl @AylinAhmet @Ayman250 @aysegulru @aysegun @Ayurveda_Today @AyurvedaSchool @ayurvediclove @az_awee @AZ_Wedding_Pros
@Azbek @AZFamilyPhoto @AZHIAZIAM4life @azjulia @azlocate @AZLotteryChicks @azquad6 @azueropanama @AzureMarcommTX @B_R_Quillen_III @B140Tweets
@b2bdata @B2Bento @B2Bmallorca @B2BMARKETING_UK @B2CMKTGInsider @b2corporate @b46u5 @baababybaa @babajive @BabakDavani @babarkamranahmd
@Babies411 @BabolatTexas @babu2480 @BabyBlooze @BabyBonanza @BabyboomerGeek @babyboomerslife @babyboomincome @BabyButterflyB @BabyChampion
@babychickdesign @BabyComplete @BabyContests @BabyDinesOut @BabyLayth @babyname4 @babyosphere @BabyReporter @babysleepmusic @BabyWebmaster

Contents

Introduction: *Everything You Ever Wanted to Know*   3
about Social Media but Were Too
Embarrassed To Ask

Part 1: *Why You Need Social Media*   9

- What Social Media Is
- How Strong It Is
- What it Delivers – For FREE
- Why You Can't Live without It

Part 2: *5-Step Plan to Positive ROI through*   21
Social Media

Chapter 1: *Shut Up and Listen!*   23

Case Study:	Mayo Clinic	31
Case Study:	James Wood Motors	36
Case Study:	Anheuser-Busch	39
Case Study:	Bodycology®	42
Case Study:	Social Media Delivered	46

Chapter 2: *Why Opposites Attract*   51

    Case Study: Lane Bryant   56

    Case Study: 21st Century Dental   62

    Case Study: Cable & Wireless Worldwide   65

    Case Study: S.M.A.R.T. Restaurant Group   68

Chapter 3: *One Ball is Not Enough to Juggle*   71

    Case Study: The Women's Museum   79

    Case Study: McDaniel Executive Recruiting   84

    Case Study: The Adolphus Hotel   87

    Case Study: Texas State Optical   91

    Case Study: General Motors   94

INSERT: *Illustrations*   101

Chapter 4: *The Social Media Equation™*   119
Chapter 5: *The ROI of Social Media*   139

Conclusion: *A Few Tough Questions*   149

Social Media for the CEO

*The Why and ROI of Social Media
for the CEO of Today and Tomorrow*

www.SocialMediafortheCEO.com

Introduction:
Everything You Ever Wanted to Know about Social Media But Were Too Embarrassed to Ask

I am a CEO and I'm guessing that, if you're not one already, you would like to be one someday. Congratulations, you've got guts, and for this brave new world, guts are certainly required.

My journey down the social media road began years ago and many people have praised me for my foresight and brilliance. They are very kind but, the truth is, what really took me down this road was DESPERATION.

A few years ago, perhaps you'll remember, the economy took a heck of a dip. It punched me in the gut. All of a sudden the things I had done well for my entire career and had been a shining executive at no longer worked. And like any professional who had a substantial amount of experience and success under her belt, **I began to fight**.

I did all the things I knew would work for sure and always had in the past, but this time nothing worked. Prospects were not calling back, no one was returning emails, and I couldn't get a deal done to save my life.

Then one day I went on LinkedIn, the largest professional social media networking site. I had been a member of LinkedIn for a long time and I can't remember *why* I logged in that day, but perhaps it was because people immediately think of LinkedIn when they are thinking about finding a new job.

I spent the next few days on LinkedIn discovering connections, industry information, and industry events but best of all, I found prospects and leads. That's when it hit me: PROSPECTS and LEADS were right there as plain as day; all I had to do was look in the right place!

And so my social media obsession began.

I spent the next few years trying to figure out this beast people called "social media," which I had for so long dismissed. Hearing the word "Twitter" simply made me giggle. It really did not make sense to me why people would join Twitter and listen to people they didn't know talk about their cats. And in the words of the great Betty White speaking about Facebook in her Saturday Night Live appearance, which was prompted by people on Facebook begging for her to host, I thought "it sounds like a huge waste of time."

But then it clicked for me. Millions of people are on social media and if millions of people are there, then there is an audience that a business could get exposure to.

And the best part? They can get exposure to these millions of people for FREE. I've always liked free things. I like to try the samples at Whole Foods and I make sure to bring home the shampoo from the hotel even if I have plenty at home just because it's FREE. As a marketing professional who is familiar with the cost of print ads, radio time and television spots, the idea of free "air time" was certainly intriguing.

Imagine that a television executive met you today and because he was in a fabulous mood decided to give you a national sixty-second spot during prime time – for FREE! What would you do with sixty seconds? Would you have your child go on live TV and talk about your company or ask someone in the office to put together a few things to say real fast? Hopefully not!

Instead, you would most likely hire a marketing company or use your own marketing team and put together a smashing concept with a fully produced commercial that entertained and informed the audience enough that participants would want to buy your product.

Apparently, the FREE-ness of social media has intrigued many a business person and so they dive in right away unprepared. Just because the vehicle of delivery is free doesn't mean there should be no preparation to embracing the fastest growing media in the history of the world – social media.

With this book, in just a few hours, you'll take a journey that took me years to walk. You'll understand the How, the Why and the ROI of Social Media with real-life case studies from companies of all sizes. Yes, there are the large companies that we can learn from showcased in this book, but there are also small- and medium-sized companies with very important and very real stories to share as well.

In this book, I'll reveal the down-to-earth truth about social media, not with complicated graphs, charts or schedules but with a very simple system in everyday language you can actually understand that I call *The Social Media Equation*™:

1.)   Shut Up and Listen! (Or, Remember, It's a Communication Tool, Not Just a Broadcast Tool.): Questions and answers – those are really all there is to social media. Your prospects and customers have questions. How do I garden without hurting my knees? How do I get a word processing program without buying the rest of the package? How do I get from Point A to Point B quicker, smarter, shorter, etc.? But if you're broadcasting all the time, sending out nothing more than digital billboards, how will you ever hear their questions?

2.)   Why Opposites Attract: If you do all the right things in the wrong place, social media will not grow your business. Many people go into social media looking to put "like with like." In other words, they join networks filled with counterparts and competitors. Don't do it! You need to go where your prospects and customers are, and that's why opposites attract.

3.)   One Ball Is Not Enough to Juggle: Have you ever watched a juggler engage a crowd by throwing around one ball? No? Of course you haven't. In the game of social media, many companies try just that. Unfortunately, when it comes to social media most people only think of one thing at a time.

4.) The Social Media Equation™: Believe it or not, there IS an equation to make sure that your social media efforts CONVERT INTO BUSINESS. This chapter not only tells you what the equation is, but walks you through it step-by-step.

5.) The ROI of Social Media: Measuring social media results can be a challenge, but it's not impossible. In fact, when you have two things – a specific goal in mind AND a way to track your progress through clearly delineated checkpoints, you actually CAN determine the return on your social media investment.

That's it. Five simple steps to total social media domination! Okay, okay, so maybe not TOTAL domination, but at least a proven and effective way to make sure that your social media efforts will lead to business growth.

Now, before we're off to the races, I want you to understand not just how to get the most out of social media but something equally important: WHY the heck you need social media in the first place.

Luckily, that's just what our next section is about.

Part 1:

Why You Need
Social Media

The other day, I was sitting outside in front of Starbucks fostering my caffeine addiction with a few friends. It wasn't too long after we'd gotten comfortable that a young man raced out, ear to his cell phone, on what was obviously a "very important" call.

It was hard not to eavesdrop, but I always like to hear how people speak on the phone because, after all, I'm in the communication business. I like to hear how people make their business case, how they sell and how they close the deal.

He was good, I'll give him that; at least good at using plenty of the latest industry buzz words. I heard "bandwidth," quite a few times, and "we need to close the loop" and a few others I'm sure were in the same vein.

Shortly, the call was over and as soon as he took his phone away from his ear he did a quick little pivot from the parking lot to face the coffee house patio.

"How is everybody doing?" he addressed our cozy little crowd.

Before we could mumble a rather surprised response, he launched into what I would call a "soliloquy." In the five brief minutes he spoke to us, we learned his name (Richard), how old he was (31), how long he'd been in town (9 months), what he did for a living (software sales consultant), who he was here with (his date, but it was "nothing serious"), her name (Camille), and what she was having (white mocha).

It wasn't what he said in this minutes-long confession that caught my attention so much as what he said when he'd had his fill and was ready to go. He shook each of our hands, looked us in the eye and said, without a trace of irony, "It was really great talking with you."

Then he disappeared, as quickly as he'd arrived.

Immediately we resumed whatever chat he'd interrupted, but his comment stuck with me all through my latte: "It was really great talking with you."

It didn't really strike me until I sat down to write this book: what bothered me about that man's statement? He wasn't talking *with us*, he was talking *at us*.

At heart, that is the frailty – and the power – of social media.

Because of all the things it isn't, social media IS a conversation. And just as with every conversation, you have a choice. Every time you use social media, you have a choice. You can either talk *at* people, or you can talk *with* people.

My job is to help you talk with people; it's called a conversation, and it's what social media is all about. But don't take my word for it, let's get into our discussion of what social media is (and isn't) right away.

What Social Media Is

What, exactly, *is* social media?

According to Wikipedia.com today, which will be different by the time you are reading this book because it gets tweaked fairly often these days, social media is "media designed to be disseminated through social interaction, created using highly accessible and scalable publishing techniques."

Hmm, sounds pretty challenging, huh? My definition is a lot simpler: **social media is simply people communicating through technology**.

Not bad, huh?

I mean, how hard can *that* be?

Well, the problem is most of us don't know how to communicate offline, let alone online! Take that snazzy young salesman in the great suit with the sleek phone who thought he was talking *with* us when, really, he was just talking *at* us.

How many conversations do you have like that per day? And not just with salesmen, but with bosses, clients, colleagues, neighbors … even friends? We're so used to talking *at* people, it's rare when we get the chance to finally talk *with* people.

Well, here's your chance. Social media is an open dialogue – in real-time with real people. Social media professionals are really just communication professionals who leverage the power of social media so that they can talk to thousands of people at a time instead of only one person at a time.

But to be fair, the real magic happens when you boil it down to one special person who interacts at a very committed level and becomes your next client. The best way to find that "magical" one person who simply can't live without your product is no different than it has been for years – start by getting your message out to thousands.

Why is social media growing so rapidly?

In my experience, the answer is fairly simple: people are eager for this one-on-one conversation, particularly with CEOs, entrepreneurs, business owners and industry leaders with knowledge that has rarely been so easily accessible in the past. People want juicy, easily digestible morsels of "byte-" sized information served up on a silver platter.

For so long, companies, businessmen, advertisers and the media have talked *at* us. Now we have a chance to talk *with* them. Historically, advertising was a one-way dialogue. Whether it was an engaging TV commercial, a 30-second radio spot, a full-page magazine spread, a direct mailer or a bench sign, marketing and PR specialized in "billboards."

Suddenly the floodgates have opened up to a two-way dialogue and people – your customers – are responding with attention verging on obsession.

Imagine a world in which the second you put your ad for toothpaste on TV you have the ability to hear from Susie, a housewife in Scranton, in her own words: "I love your mint toothpaste, my family's used it for years, but your cinnamon toothpaste is too hot – and it leaves little red bumps all over my sink."

Could you imagine? Forget focus groups and test markets and tastings and surveys, you now have the ability to get real-time data from your actual customers **in their own words**.

It's not science fiction. It's social media.

The best part? This kind of open-ended dialogue happens in real-time, every day, all over the web. If you're not mastering social media, you're missing out on this essential form of modern communication.

How Strong It Is

How strong is social media?

Let me put it this way: If Facebook were a country, it would be the **third most populated country in the world**.

Social media is the fastest growing type of media in the history of the world. How fast? Too fast for it to be practical for me to put the latest statistics into a book that will come out a few months after I type these very words. (For the very latest numbers, I suggest you visit

Mashable.com, the "bible" of all things social media.)

Meanwhile, here are some staggering facts:

- Social media is the number-one activity on the web now – overtaking pornography.

- It took radio 38 years to reach 50 million users.

- It took television 13 years to reach 50 million users.

- It took the internet four years to reach 50 million users.

- It took Facebook nine months to reach 100 million users.

To let these amazing statistics (plus plenty more) sink in, go to YouTube.com and search "Socialnomics" to watch Erik Qualman's videos that get the point across.

What It Delivers

I talk with CEOs all the time and when I mention something like Facebook or Twitter, they almost immediately say, "Yes, my (wife/husband/child/mom/friend) is on that and wastes all their time there, but what does that have to do with my business?"

Great answer! Why? Simply, the client has already begun to argue my case for me. For any effective marketing and communication process to work, first of all, **you have to get people there**. Guess what? When it comes to social media, they are already there and the rest of the world is running there quickly to catch up.

I also tell clients with small or medium companies to pay attention to the last five seconds of nearly every ad you see on TV, look at the bottom of every article you read on Inc.com or in *Newsweek*, look in the corner of every magazine ad you'll read today and you'll see one consistent message: "Find us on Twitter and Facebook."

Do you know how much it costs per second to be on national TV? Or how valuable space is in a print or online ad? All I know is that the last time I checked it cost a whole lot of money.

So why in the world would Tide or Coca-Cola or John Deere or Target waste valuable TV or ad copy time asking you to join them on Twitter and Facebook? The answer: they value your communication or, at least, the chance to communicate *with* you.

But enough about communication, let's talk about **delivery**.

In other words, what can social media do for YOU? How can it deliver the value for your time, energy and constant maintenance of this social media machine?

What, in the end, is your ROI going to be?

I'll keep the answer(s) simple and direct. Here are the three things social media delivers:

1.) Customer Service   2.) Marketing   3.) Communication

Most people in social media are doing one or maybe two of these fundamentals, but not all three. Social media has the potential to deliver all three things, not just one or the other. So if you're only talking about customer service, that's great, but you're missing a huge opportunity when it comes to marketing and communication.

If you're only marketing your product through social media, you're only getting a third of the way down the road. If you are only focusing on communicating, then you will be losing out on opportunities to serve your customers and to promote your offerings.

When you combine these three deliverables, they are exponentially more effective. The reason that all three are more effective is the same reason that when you take a holistic approach to running your business and growing your company, it comes together and works.

Imagine a strategy meeting to move your company forward when you only invite one or two divisions; it's a lopsided effort that, frankly, is bound to fail.

Most CEOs understand the power that each department adds to the foundation and the possibilities of synergy when they all move in the same direction. The same applies for this new tool, social media.

Social media is simply a tool; the world of business has not changed. So use this tool to increase customer service, marketing and communication and you'll start seeing business results at an exponential rate that you haven't experienced in many years.

Why You Can't Live without It

Why can't you live without social media?

Imagine living without … the internet.

Imagine living without … email.

Imagine living without television, airplanes, a microwave or the radio.

Once upon a time, all of these things – from TV to microwave ovens to the internet – were thought of as "fads" that wouldn't stand the test of time.

The social media conversation has already begun.

It's going on right now.

Your prospects are already there and so are your competitors. Even Ellen DeGeneres is already there!! Seriously, though, of course you CAN survive without social media, but you can probably also survive with your company making a lot less money. Why would you want to?

Take a look down the road two years from now. Can you really afford to miss out on the competitive edge for two long years?

Imagine not having a website for the next two years, or not allowing customers to shop online, or blocking emails. Social media is a conversation and people are talking about you NOW – with or without you. You want to be part of the conversation – sooner rather than later. This book will help you share your message, loud and clear.

Part 2:

5-Step Plan to Positive ROI through Social Media

Chapter 1:
Shut Up and Listen!

Remember the old adage "If a tree falls in the forest and no one is there, does it really make a sound?" Many executives treat their organization's online reputation like this.

They stay out of the forest and think that if they don't hear the tree then it won't matter. The only problem is the forest of social media is already populated with millions of people. When a sound is made, they hear it, whether you're there or not.

You might think the very first step to succeeding in social media is to immediately start talking. After all, that's what everybody else seems to be doing, right? Talking about their industries, their companies and their products and services?

Wrong. Now is not the time to start talking; now is the time, to put it bluntly, to **shut up** and **listen**. Right now, somewhere, probably in a lot of places, people are talking about you, your brand, your organization, your cause, your product, your service and your competitors.

The conversation is already taking place; you are powerless to prevent it from happening. People will talk about you, your industry, your products and services; the only way to stay relevant to the conversation – and potentially influence it – is to show up and hear what everybody is already saying.

The very first step to effective social media is simply to listen.

How? How can you possibly "listen in" on the thousands of conversations that are taking place about your industry, your company, and your products every day?

There are many methods of free (such as RSS, Search.Twitter.com, Google Alerts) and paid technology you can leverage to hear what people are saying about you. These tools are used every day, and they are always changing.

The most important thing you can do before you begin listening is to understand the climate of three critical areas:

1.) **Your industry**
2.) **Your company**
3.) **Your product(s)/service(s)**

Listen For What People Are Saying about Your Industry

Begin by listening to what people are saying about your industry in general. Your industry is a world unto its own, whether you work in heavy machinery, fashion, publishing, greeting cards, scented markers, holiday socks or cosmetics.

Every industry has a lingo, a feel, a mode, a tone, an arc and new trends. Join industry groups on LinkedIn or Facebook, follow the popular industry blogs, devote a fraction of every day simply honing in on your industry and what the general tone is. Get the feel for it to understand the hot topics, things that matter, things that people are passionate about, and controversial developments.

Why should we listen to what others in our industry have to say about our industry? Why should we care what our competitors think about this trend or that technology?

Many times what we think is important to the industry is, in fact, considered rather insignificant by others in the industry – let alone our customers. Keeping your finger on the industry in general lets you know where you stand in comparison with others.

Listen For What People Are Saying about Your Company

Next, drill down deeper to hear what people are saying specifically about your organization or brand. Remember, you're not here to post your own rants or comment on user comments, but just to listen to what the mood is toward your company at this moment in time.

Google yourself! Bing yourself! (It's not as dirty as it sounds!)

Now do the same for your company, your product.

You can also search for your name and company name on Facebook.com, Twitter.com, YouTube.com, LinkedIn.com and find what people are saying in two clicks or less.

Whatever method you choose, this is a great way to find out what folks are really saying about your company … and NOT just the folks you pay to say things about your company.

In nearly every organization there is the *perception* of how others feel about your company and what folks *really* feel about your company. When the Sci-Fi Channel switched to SyFy, I remember reading a profile about the company's head honchos and the spin that was put on things within – and perhaps even by – corporate headquarters. Walking away from the article, I truly felt like the name change was a great decision.

Then I googled "SyFy" and learned what people *outside* the company felt. The perceptions couldn't have been more different if they were night and day: fans were irate, industry insiders were doubtful, TV and cable columnists considered it "wasteful."

It's important to remember that the things you, your department heads, managers and even employees consider so clever, unique, different and valuable can be seen quite differently not only by others in your industry and your competitors, but by potential customers as well. In fact, even the opinions and carefully crafted ads you've sent out may or may not match the reality of the mindset of your customers.

How will you ever know if you don't listen?

Listen For What People Are Saying about Your Products and Services

Finally, the last step is to take a deep, long, careful look at what people are saying about your products and services, and compare that to what they are saying about your competitors' products.

Read the comments on your company website, read your product reviews on Amazon.com (and while you're there, you should probably write a great review about this book!), follow your products in the local and national media, and don't read the rave reviews more often than you do the jeers.

I liken this step to going to counseling, where someone who is an objective party sits you down and tells you your faults, weaknesses and gives you a valid opinion that isn't designed to protect – or hurt – your feelings but is, instead, designed to tell you the unvarnished truth. It's not always pretty and it's not very fun, but the knowledge you gain can change the way you go to market forever.

It's important to remember the reason social media is the most powerful and fastest-growing media in the history of the world: it's not just that the technology has enabled free and instant delivery, it's about the **human need to communicate**. And as anyone who is a communications expert will tell you, the best and most effective communication comes from **listening first**.

Why go to all this trouble?

The reason for all this listening and gathering of information is for you to get a clear picture of where you stand before getting started. This is a foundation from which you can create a valid and authentic social media presence in the *real* world, as opposed to the presence you thought you had. Listening will help you bridge that gap between perception and reality.

It's a little like buying a new outfit, trying it on and asking your grandmother what she thinks about it. Perhaps your grandmother – a sweet, elderly, gray-haired woman who loves you and would never, ever want to hurt your feelings – tells you it's "gorgeous, simply gorgeous."

Meanwhile, there are women like *my* grandmother. "Honies" was a beauty queen in the 1930s with an impeccable sense of fashion, which somehow skipped over me genetically. These kinds of grandmothers love you just as much as the other ones, but don't want to see you looking like a fool, so they offer you a much more realistic (and perhaps unpleasant) opinion. You need people like this who will tell it like it is. Then, you have to have the guts to consider making the change.

In other words, it's important to celebrate the positive feedback you get, but not to the exclusion of the negative. When you know what people are REALLY saying about you, you're in a better position to craft a social media campaign that will actually have a shot at breaking through.

It's important to celebrate the positive feedback you get, but it's even more important to **listen to the criticism**. When you know what people are REALLY saying about you, you're in a better position to craft a social media campaign that is credible because it is rooted in reality.

The Risk of Not Being at the Party

Here is how I like to describe social media to my clients. Let's say there's a great big party happening and everybody is going. All of your clients, your prospects and even your competitors will be there.

You're going, right?

What's that?

You're NOT going?

You're staying home instead?

Hmmm, that's not such a great idea. After all, this "party" is social media, and everybody is talking anyway, so what will you lose by not listening? What will you miss when your customers say things you should know about your product or service, but aren't there to hear? Why would you let your competitors be privy to that information while you stay at home and put your feet up? They may very well be listening.

The folks who get to this party early get a better spot; those who don't show up get left in the dust. That is social media; that is why it's so important. Specifically, that is why listening is such an important part of social media.

Case Study # 1: Mayo Clinic

Organization: Mayo Clinic; MayoClinic.org

Background: Mayo Clinic is a not-for-profit medical practice dedicated to the diagnosis and treatment of virtually every type of complex illness.

Business Need: To leverage the Mayo Clinic's established reputation in direct promotion, rather than relying only on third-party media representation. In short, "Don't just pitch the media, *be* the media."

Social Media Solution: A custom YouTube channel, which serves as an excellent platform to distribute syndicated press package videos created for traditional TV news and information to the media parties interested in featuring the Mayo Clinic. Furthermore, the YouTube channel became a place for amateur and casual videos (See page 104).

Business Result: Very large numbers of viewers (currently over 2 million) means a lot of exposure. Thanks to low production costs on many of the clips, any return on investment is significant. This channel has become a destination within itself and a way for Mayo Clinic to leverage its reputation without having to always use a third party.

What actually happened:

Lee Aase, Manager, Syndication and Social Media at Mayo Clinic points out that for over 100 years the Mayo Clinic has relied almost completely on word of mouth and third-party media to spread its reputation. As social media is the new word of mouth, the various platforms available fit in perfectly with the clinic's traditional means of promotion. Plus, it affords the Mayo Clinic the opportunity to use its own reputation to its advantage.

As Mr. Aase stated, "Don't just pitch the media, be the media," meaning the Mayo Clinic has a very strong reputation, and does not have to rely solely on third-party media representation to establish credibility. They already have a lot of credibility in their field, and can use that as a way to appeal to a wider audience.

In addition, because the clinic is a not-for-profit organization, there is less pressure to see an immediate return on investment, and more opportunity to use social media in a purely altruistic sense. Of course, this also brings greater social media success, because social media is often about sharing valuable information.

The implementation of a YouTube channel provides the clinic with another platform to utilize the 90-second to 2-minute syndicated press package videos created for traditional TV news and information to the media parties interested in featuring Mayo Clinic, and creates a platform to pitch to traditional media. It also reinforces the clinic's established reputation by providing information and advice to patient communities, and speeds up the dissemination of medical information on rare or specialized illnesses to people across the world at a rate never experienced before. Though there is not as strong a focus on ROI as there might be in a corporation, Mr. Aase explains that the clinic still sees new patients coming in because of content they viewed on the Mayo Clinic YouTube channel.

A perfect example is the 10-½-minute video of Dr. Mesa discussing myelofibrosis, a rare form of blood cancer, which was shot with a simple $150 Flip camera. This video has been viewed more than 4,000 times. Dr. Mesa has heard from over 50 out-of-state patients who chose Mayo Clinic because they saw his video and asked specifically for Dr. Mesa. Not only does this video provide necessary information to potential patients, the clinic's ROI from making that information widely available through YouTube is substantial.

One key element in the clinic's social media strategy is the inter-connectedness across platforms. Mayo Clinic runs a Twitter feed, Facebook page, YouTube channel and several blogs, and Mr. Aase says these different channels are all crucial to a successful social media campaign.

In July 2010, Mayo Clinic increased its commitment to using social media by creating the Mayo Clinic Center for Social Media. The center's purpose is to go beyond the public relations and marketing uses of social media, and to use variations of these tools throughout the organization. Through the center, Mayo aims to accelerate adoption of social media in the clinical practice, education, research and administration.

The center's focus is not only internal to Mayo Clinic, however. The center also will be a resource for other hospitals and health-related organizations looking for guidance in applying social media. "Many staff in health care organizations who are interested in using social media have pointed to our Mayo Clinic example to help make their case to leadership," Mr. Aase explains. "Through the center we have a way for them to join a formal network, and to get access to materials and resources to support their venture into social media."

Mr. Aase says the network will not be limited to medical providers, but also will include non-profit health related organizations and associations. "We want to be a resource to any organization looking for ways to apply social media to improve health," he says. "Our fundamental goal is to help patients through social media, whether that means giving them increased access to scientific information or

@denverpolitics @denverpost @DenverPostPicks @DenverPR @denverrei @denversnowdude @denversolarguy @DenverTwitr @denyseduhaime @deolonline @dconderneemster @Deoxydoesit @Departer @depressividade @Derek_Haines @derekantoncich @DerekBrad @derekjoesoto @dereklacroix @dereksemmler @DerekTampa @DerfMagazine @Deri_light @Dermacut @Dermaxin @DeRosaImports @derrickcarlisle @Derricktodd @DerrolConnor @desdealbert0 @DesdeCantera @DesertRealtors @DesertSunNudist @deshocks @desigg @desigink @design_crawley @design_more01 @Design_Pro @Design4people @designandvoip @DesignDolceVita @designdune @designer_sarah @designerchoc @DesignerDepot @DesignerG @DesignerSecrets @designfollow @DesignsbyKoko @designstormgirl @Designstudiouk @designtourney @designtwit @DesireePaquette @DesireeScales @DeslockDarkstar @DesmondChild @desole @DesperateHighwa @DesperatHighway @DessertsRecipes @DestDaily @destinynefx @destockmode @DeStressCDs @detaildevils @DetailXPerts @determineddirk @Determinism @detobey @detourshirts @DetoxTips @detrick @Detroit_ Alerts @detroitautoblog @DetroitPR @DetVendetta @DeuceProCEO @deuhlig @deusexcomputer @deutche @DeutscheOnline @DeVeauDunn @deveshd @Devils_Workday @Devindelane @devinemarketing @devinhunter @devinjoncarlson @devKhalid @devon_jordan @devonbrown @devongall @DevonSkinner @DevoraRhoads @Devoted2HR @Dew95 @dewhurst4texas @Dewydeeee @DexterAddict @dexteralbrecht @DexterJr5 @DezignersDen @dfarnsworth1 @DFBrouillette @dferreira @DFHanna @dfkom @dflanegan @dfolkens @dfrieson @DFW_ATTORNEY @dfw_dance @DFW_HOMES @DFW_Joblist @DFW_Mama @dfwama @DFWAreaCadillac @DFWAssistant @dfwbargames @dfwbars @dfwbizlink @DFWcon @DFWDANCE @DFWDanceTalk @DFWGuide @DFWHIPHOPEVENTS @DFWHomeRentals @DFWHotBizTalk @DFWLeaders @DFWMoneyMatters @dfwreupdate @DFWSOCIALMEDIA @DFWStuff @DFWTRN @dfwvideo @dfwwp @dg @dgcbooth @DGGT @DGilabert @DGL45 @Dgreatone @dgupta5150 @DHA_2010 @dhanimu @dhanishth @dharmacharya @DharmaTalks @DHarmer4USHouse @dharrison47 @dhatfield @dhayes3396 helping them to get together and learn from each other, becoming active partners with their health care providers. We also want to help medical professionals in research and education connect with each other, and are eager to play a role in spreading the use of these powerful communication tools throughout the health system."

For more information about the Mayo Clinic Center for Social Media, go to SocialMedia.MayoClinic.org.

Case Study # 2: James Wood Motors

Organization: James Wood Motors; JamesWood.com

Background: James Wood Motors consists of several car dealerships with numerous brands located in Denton and Decatur, Texas, close to the Dallas area.

Business Need: Build more relationships with prospects that prefer to shop virtually.

Social Media Solution: Develop a Twitter campaign to be used as an information resource for potential customers (See page 105).

Business Result: Increased sales as a direct result from Twitter interactions and grew online reputation by customers sharing positive reviews on Yelp®.

What actually happened:

In early 2009, the management at James Wood Motors hypothesized that using one or several social media vehicles might aid them in connecting with potential customers and helping them to make car-purchasing decisions.

They decided to provide a wealth of information

through Twitter at Twitter.com/JamesWoodMotors. "We communicate different things with Twitter," says Amanda Williams, Internet Director at James Wood Motors. "From up-to-the-minute new vehicle arrivals to community involvement projects, inside views of operations, behind the scenes, even interaction with moms test-driving our vehicles."

Additionally, social media allows James Wood Motors to bridge the gap that exists between their geographic location and their customer base that works and resides all over the Dallas-Fort Worth-Denton area.

Adds Williams, "We use Twitter to communicate with our customers who use it as a way to maintain distance while shopping for vehicles. Not everyone is comfortable shopping for vehicles, we know that. In today's times, people are more at ease keeping their distance and using a site like Twitter. We send pictures, exchange info via direct message, video, etc. The customers obtain the info they need."

By sharing information about their dealership and relevant product information via Twitter, James Wood Motors caught the attention of Mr. Colin Burns, a marketing professional looking to purchase a new car.

Burns was so moved after pleasantly interacting with James Wood Motors throughout the buying process, that he felt compelled to submit a Yelp review praising the experience he had at the dealership, with their staff and with the car itself:

> "Amanda from @jameswoodmotors was a HUGE help. It was nice to have someone quickly respond to my questions on Twitter with pictures, information about the car, if they worked with my bank, etc. ... I was able to do all my homework on the back end to figure out that I was getting a good deal and left the entire process 100% comfortable with the car I had picked and the price I was paying. If I could do it all over again I'd do it the same way – shop on Twitter, see it in real life, make the purchase."

In addition to social media, James Wood Motors continues to use traditional methods of advertising such as billboards, radio and television. Social media has offered them a less expensive and surprisingly effective addition to the marketing mix. Owner James Wood commented, "Our business has always been about building relationships and if social media can speed that up for us, then it is definitely a smart business decision."

Case Study # 3: Anheuser-Busch

Organization: Anheuser-Busch Companies, Inc; Anheuser -Busch.com

Background: Anheuser-Busch is a global brewer that produces the world's largest-selling beers, Budweiser and Bud Light.

Business Need: Create more community with sports fans

Social Media Solution: A news/story-style video of sports fans on YouTube (See page 106).

Business Results: Their efforts resulted in an Emmy-award-winning program for 2010 that yielded massive fan audience and interaction.

What actually happened:

Bud Light wanted to build participation and interaction with passionate sports fans, and they turned to Chris Yates and Jim Knox at Huddle Productions, where they understood that the habits of television viewers had changed. Nowadays, fans wanted to watch video whenever they wanted and as soon as possible. However, viewers not only wanted a story – they wanted to be PART of the story.

With this approach, Huddle Productions created "GameDay Rivals," an interactive social media campaign focused on filming football fans and their unique traditions and quirky rituals. Tailgaters from all over the U.S. competed during football season to be crowned Bud Light's Ultimate Tailgate Fan.

Huddle Productions filmed the fans at stadiums then shared the videos on social sites like YouTube, Facebook and Twitter. Fans voted, commented, created and engaged one another, thus creating a conversation frenzy all season long. This was the kind of unique marketing and direct interaction with their fans that Anheuser-Busch wanted.

Consequently, the GameDay Rivals program won the 2010 Emmy Award for the "Best Sport Program of the Year." Their concept of engaging fans and the use of video in social media generated the following results:

STATS Increase Year 1 to Year 2:

- **750,000 votes**   **+1200%**

- **417,087 website video views**   **+522%**

- **1600 Facebook fans**   **+144%**

- **113,900 YouTube views**   **+60%**

"GameDay Rivals in search of Bud Light's Ultimate Tailgater was one of the most successful local marketing campaigns. It was creative and effective," said Jay Black, the Director of Marketing at Anheuser-Busch InBev. "We are always looking at trying new and innovative ways to market and Huddle Productions did that with this concept."

Case Study # 4: Bodycology®

Organization: Bodycology with Advanced Beauty Systems; Bodycology.com

Background: Bodycology is a product line developed by Dallas-based Advanced Beauty Systems. Their beauty products are designed to be "spa-quality" and intended for women who want "beauty on a budget."

Business Need: An online interactive experience for Bodycology's users

Social Media Solution: Use interactive banners to create a strong CTA or call to action (See page 107).

Business Result: Development of a massive consumer email database, which was subsequently used to create My|Bodycology®, an interactive health and beauty portal containing blogs, quizzes and product resources.

What actually happened:

In 2009, Bodycology had recently launched an offline campaign centered around a simple question: "What's Your Bodycology?" Bodycology's interactive agency, Boxcar Creative, saw this as a promising online opportunity, and defined a strategy to leverage the offline campaign into a strong online interactive campaign with their potential consumers.

This strategy had two key features:

1.) Incorporate a strong call to action (CTA) to generate data for their consumer database, with particular emphasis on contact information collection.

2.) Actively respond to user behavior by creating an interactive resource for the consumers.

A clear CTA is vital to any marketing campaign. The online initiative began with a banner campaign composed of both standard (non-interactive) and interactive banner types. Both the standard and the interactive banner types had a clear, simple CTA ("Take quiz"). Once prompted by the CTA, the interactive units provided the user with the ability to take the quiz within the banner, as well as submit an email address, while the standard banners drove users to a landing page with the same quiz/email capture functionality.

The "What's Your Bodycology?" banner campaign netted nearly 40,000 email addresses in less than eight weeks. The interaction rate was 24.29%, far surpassing the industry standard interaction rate of 7.64%. The conversion rate from visits to email sign-ups was 6% – the high end of the industry rate, which is between 1% and 6%.

Having 40,000 unexpected email addresses inspired the next steps, which would ultimately be used to create My|Bodycology®. A challenge was extended to the email database, wherein emails were blasted out to users, encouraging women to vote on their top areas of interest. The potential areas of content included: Fitness, Beauty Tips, Celebrities, Health/Wellness, Fashion, Value, Parenting, Household Tips, Horoscopes, Nutrition, Finances, Success Stories, Editorial. The voting was a fun, interactive way to connect the brand with its users.

Presently, Bodycology® has their top six areas as generated by their users:

1.) Nutrition

2.) Finance

3.) Fitness

4.) Value

5.) Entertainment

6.) Household Tips

Phase 1 of My|Bodycology® launched in summer 2010. It included blogs from various women on the aforementioned topics as well as quizzes and product information. My|Bodycology® is a result of Bodycology's active response to the user's behavior, and will serve as the online arena to be controlled by the user. An agenda can't be forced in the process of developing such an arena. All a company can do for its consumers is give them a clear CTA and be sure to respond accordingly.

Case Study # 5: Social Media Delivered

Organization: Social Media Delivered, LLC

Background: Eve Mayer Orsburn is an executive who decided to use social media to create a business doing social media for other organizations.

Business Need: As a vital part of meeting the client's need, Eve decided to brand herself on social media first, then build business through social media before reaching out to clients and doing the same for them. Eve reasoned that if she could create an enormous social media presence for herself first, she could point to her own success as a great example of what she could do for clients.

Social Media Solution: Create an optimized profile for Eve Mayer Orsburn at LinkedIn.com/in/EveMayerOrsburn and use the largest professional network to create and grow a new business. It was then imperative to build an entire company and fulfill almost every need through social media (See pages 108 and 109).

Business Result: SocialMediaDelivered.com became one of the largest social media optimization companies worldwide with a thriving client list garnered through social media in

@EzBuyPerfumes @EZClickbankcash @ezcreditrepair1 @EzihAlive @EzineProfits @ezonlineincome @EZPayroll @ezPoachedEggs @EZSportsPicks @ezwealthman @ezwealthmlm @ezwealthmoney @ezwealthtaxi @ezyhelper @f0nesex @F4binhosk8 @fabfas @fabianalaura @FabianKern @FabianTan @FabKimberly @FabLifeHacker @FabriceCathala @FabulousAndFit @facebook4u @FacebookBiz_4u @FacebookPetitio @FacebookPro @Facethesunmovie @factpile @fadeyifemi @FadiSemaan @faethefirst @faffiliate @fafnews @fahadzaheer @fahrradel @failingenglish @FailWhaleBook @FairfieldDesign @FairmontDallas @FairyBlogMother @fairygirl111 @faisalmasoodCOM @faisk @faistech @faithfulpoet @faithgoddess17 @faithpeterson @faithworks2005 @faiyzy @FajarHudhiarto @fak3r @fakebelieve @fakecongressman @FakeHowardDean @fakeresume @fakeself @FallowfieldsUK @FallyneJ @FamHealthGuide @familybandb @FamilyeGuide @FamilyFrolic @familylink @FamilyMatters01 @FamilyOwned @famlovejustin08 @Famous_Daves @FamousFootwear @fancylisting @fantabulousfran @FantasticBooks @Fantasy_Brain @FAQShop @farahato @farecoup @farenda9 @FarFlungMedia @farhatkhan22 @FarmerHaley @farmvillekid @farmvilleyoda @farotto @farrah77 @FarrellHeyworth @farroutphoto @fasblog @Fashion_Guru_NZ @FashionAccess @Fashionali @FashioNBR9 @FashionBuddah @FashionCentsMom @fashionguru222 @FashionInq @FashionistasB @fashionnowpuh @fashions_styles @Fashions4Flirts @FashionSession @fast_thinking @FasTake @fastcarmoney @fastcompany @FastComputerlpc @fasterfollow @fastfatlose @fastfatloss @FastFingers_VA @fastglobalnews @FastHomeBuyers @FastMoneySystem @FastMuscleGain @FastrackMedia @fastrentals @FastTweets @Fat_Loss_Queen @FATAFATY @fatburn247 @fatBuzz_Malcolm @Fathead @FatherPeter @fatimah_tolga @FatLoss_Help @fatlosscheetah @FatlossForEver @fatmancunian @fatmandiaries @FatNoggin @fatoskarahasan @fattachepills @fatwallet @FatWireSoftware @FaulknerStrat @faultlinellc @faultlineusa @Faux_Joe_Moore @fauxpanels @FavoriteTickets @FavorSA @FavorsbyDorinda @FawnKey @faybe @faydra_deon @fazhiiOn_Giirl @fbrglssmnfsto @FC_Barca_Fan the U.S., Canada and Europe.

What actually happened:

As a "solopreneur," Eve Mayer Orsburn began to build a presence on LinkedIn that would showcase her ability to find clients on the largest professional networking site. At first, her clients were B2B companies needing help specifically on LinkedIn.

These were primarily engineers, lawyers, speakers, coaches, non-profit organizations, medical device companies and training companies **who all began seeing results** as Eve trained their executive and sales teams on using LinkedIn. Once she achieved results, she asked these clients to spread the word with recommendations of her services on LinkedIn, then reached out to new prospects via LinkedIn groups.

Eve wanted to share her social media tips on a daily basis so she started using the address Twitter.com/LinkedInQueen, where she could share social media tips several times a day. These tips were designed to a.) ignite a passion for social media in individuals who wanted to "do it themselves" and b.) promote her services to individuals who would rather hire someone else to perform social media duties for them instead.

As her client list grew, Eve used Craigslist.com and

LinkedIn.com to hire her first employees. Suddenly Eve was no longer a solopreneur but indeed a company now known as "Social Media Delivered," which meant she needed a CPA, a mentor, representatives and companies to partner with, all of whom she found through Twitter and LinkedIn. When Eve wanted to highlight the presence of Social Media Delivered in Dallas, she started up the group Meetup.com/SocialMediaDelivered and held free networking events where she could speak on social media and turn those online connections into in-person opportunities that, in turn, would lead to more business.

More companies were coming to Social Media Delivered (SMD) and asking for help, and for the first time, they were not all B2B companies. Restaurants, hotels, hospitals, dentists, weight loss and retail companies were all B2C companies wanting to understand tools like Twitter, Facebook, YouTube, blogs and more.

To spread the messages to executives in a way that was non-technical but focused on business, SMD began posting blogs on social media for business at SocialMediaDelivered.com and shared their own social media tidbits at Twitter.com/SocialMediaDel and Facebook.com/SocialMediaDel.

Marketing companies and ad agencies noticed the talents of Social Media Delivered and began to reach out and ask for help with their own clients. Then came an online radio show "Social Media for the CEO" (SM4CEO.com) where companies of all sizes told their stories of growing business through social media.

As the company grew, more employees were brought on through social media, and more clients in the U.S., Canada and Europe searched out Social Media Delivered for their services.

In your hands now, you hold a book that is a product of this journey. The people, companies, stories, printing and publishing were all brought together purely through the power of social media and the connections made through that journey.

The journey will continue and you are already a part of it. So are the 28,000 names appearing at the bottom of the pages within this book, all of which came from Twitter.com/LinkedinQueen. Readers will post reviews about this book on Amazon.com and tweet questions/ feedback. So continues the social media trail that started with just one person then found its way to you.

Anyone can do this on any topic. Social media levels the playing field. How? Simply give more often than take, offer value and then ask for help. It will work. This case study proves it.

Chapter 2:
Why Opposites Attract

Meet Jacob.

Jacob is a man who wants to date a great woman.

Jacob has a very clear goal in his mind – *Get a great woman to agree to go out with me*. Jacob is an intelligent man and understands a great woman won't magically appear anytime soon in his living room and he must "get out there" and meet people to find her.

Jacob heads out for a night on the town to find *exactly* what he is looking for. Jacob walks down to the area where the nice establishments are known to be and is surprised to see two doors clearly marked.

One doors says, "Enter here to find a room full of great men."

The other door says, "Enter here to find a room full of great women."

Based on his stated goal, Jacob's choice *should* be pretty easy at this point.

Jacob enters the door marked "great men" and spends the evening talking to men just like himself, but at the end of the night he goes home without achieving his goal of meeting a great woman and he feels frustrated.

What? Wait a minute – how did this go wrong? Jacob's goal was so clear! How could he mess that up?

If you were a man looking for a great woman, which room would *you* enter?

"Surely," you say, "the answer is obvious: you enter the room marked 'full of great women.' " However, when people engage in social media, they often **enter the wrong room**.

So why do so many of us enter the virtual rooms or online groups in social media full of people **just like us** where very few or none of our prospects are likely to be? I know why I did it; it was less scary, I was familiar with the groups and the people … it was just plain easier to walk in and feel comfortable there – virtually speaking, of course.

Plus, when you first get into social media it's a great place to start. A place where you can see what your peers and counterparts are saying, a place where you can get educated on your industry and it's almost exactly like the way you're using social media in your personal life.

We're not talking about your personal life, we're talking about growing your business. Using social media personally and for your business are two very, very different worlds. I'm pretty sure you're going to have a tough time exponentially growing your business by only selling to people **you already know**.

To build a successful business, you must introduce your brand and product to the world. Spreading your brand to the world using only traditional media can cost a lot of money.

That's why for a small business especially, social media is a more effective way to reach the world. And to do that, you have to get in front of people **who don't know you**. This is why you must join groups that are full of your prospects, rather, the opposite of you.

Pick the Right Room!

Let me explain this concept a little more fully by using a real-life example. We work with several executive coaches, consulting with them on how to use social media to reach more prospects and gain more clients. Typically, the executive coaches would join lots of groups on Facebook and LinkedIn labeled with terms like "executive coaching group" or "professional group for coaching."

Seems logical, right?

After all, this enables them to keep up with what their competition is doing as well as stay current with evolving trends in the coaching industry. However, after spending hours of time discussing, debating or posting in these groups, they find no effect on their bottom line or build-up of their business.

Why? Because they entered the room full of great men when

they were looking for a great woman. In other words, they went into a room full of people just like them, looking to do the exact same thing, instead of going into a room full of the people they wanted to attract, i.e., potential customers.

Why Opposites Attract

When you are leveraging social media, it's important to remember that opposites attract. Although it's okay to join a few groups to keep up with your industry, make like-minded connections and follow trends, make sure the **majority** of your groups comprise your prospects.

For instance:

- **If you're an executive coach, join groups full of ... executives.**

- **If your company sells gardening tools, join groups full of ... gardeners.**

- **If you're a person who sells health insurance to HR departments, join groups full of ... HR directors.**

- **If your company sells sports drinks, join groups full of ... athletes.**

You get the picture. Yes, it seems logical to join groups full of folks who make sports drinks, but do you really think they're ever going to buy your sports drink? You have to go where the sports drink guzzlers are, not the makers!

The point is, while it's important to use social media to keep in touch with those in your industry, there are only so many hours in the day and only so many resources you can throw at social media.

Don't you want the time you DO spend to count?

This way you'll be the one great guy in a room full of eligible women.

Now your chances are much better of attracting what you want.

Why? Because you chose the right door!

So, what happens when you DO choose the right door? Getting back to our real-life example, when the executive coaches began to join large numbers of groups with executives in them, they started to post case studies showing how executive coaching was able to move an executive forward.

These were small, short, informal "success stories" – and they worked! Since our executive coaches were the minority in a select group discussing what could help the majority, the result was immediate and led to a dramatic and marked increase in business and profits.

Case Study # 6: Lane Bryant

Organization: Lane Bryant, Inc.

Background: One of the most significant women's retail clothing store chains focusing on plus-size clothing, headquartered in Columbus, Ohio, and founded in 1901 by Lena Himmelstein Bryant Malsin.

Business Need: Create a place where plus-size women could connect with each other and share their passions. Connect those passions with the Lane Bryant brand.

Social Media Solution: "The Inside Curve," which resides on LaneBryant.com and is solely dedicated to and designed for the Lane Bryant customer. Within this network, a registered member can shop, read the latest Lane Bryant buzz and connect with other members over their love for Lane Bryant and fashion (See page 110).

Business Result: A platform to address the Lane Bryant customer and inform them of a seemingly "double standard" that was being applied to Lane Bryant's TV spot by ABC and FOX TV networks. This posting on Inside Curve started the wildfire that turned into controversy online, on television and print, which equaled huge PR gains for Lane Bryant.

What actually happened:

When Jay Dunn began working with Lane Bryant as VP of Marketing, he immediately identified that the customer base Lane Bryant was trying to reach was being neglected by mainstream American advertising. Because typical U.S. retail ads didn't feature curvier women and instead focused on highlighting waif-like models, more voluptuous women had a fairly narrow menu of places where they could shop.

With this knowledge and observation, Dunn began planning a solution that would fill the need to engage the Lane Bryant customer, and generate a worthy conversation between customer and brand largely focused on what many of the customers were already talking about: the under-representation of plus-size women in America.

In 2008, Dunn and his marketing team conceived, built and incorporated into the marketing strategy a fully interactive online community network called "Inside Curve," which is solely dedicated to and designed for the Lane Bryant customer. Within this network a registered member can shop, read the latest Lane Bryant buzz and connect with other members over their love for Lane Bryant and fashion.

On April 20, 2010, Lane Bryant's marketing staff posted a 377-word blog within the company's online community network, "Inside Curve," which had approximately 30,000 devotees. The topic of the post read as follows: "The Lingerie Commercial FOX and ABC Didn't Want Its Viewers to See," and complained (quite controllably, might I add) about the recent problem the brand had faced when presenting a certain TV commercial announcing the rollout of "Cacique," the intimates line now available from Lane Bryant, to FOX and ABC.

By that evening, with 198 "Love Its," 54 comments, and a reporter from *AdWeek* now covering it – a media war had started. At the end of the blog post, readers faced crossing a "retail line in the sand" and Lane Bryant was encouraging them to pick a side: ***"Team Cacique or Team Network. Tell us how you feel and pass this along to everyone who shares the view that beauty is in the eye of the beholder not the hands of a television network."***

The Battle of Lingerie had begun ...

On Wednesday the story continued to gain momentum and showed no signs of stopping as the headline swept through Twitter, the blogosphere, and across the radio. Reporters, Jay Leno, and loyal Lane Bryant fans all wanted an answer to the same question: ***"If Victoria's Secret and Playtex can run ads at any time, [on any network] during the 9pm to 10pm hour ... Why is Lane Bryant restricted only to the*** *final 10 minutes?"*

And on Thursday, April 22, when the *New York Post* ran an article featuring the story and exposing the "visual" in question, two things were abundantly clear: Team Cacique had scored MAJOR support points from across the nation and, more importantly, in the new Era of Social Media Networking, a mere 377 words could create quite an impact.

By raising awareness about the issue within a smaller but dedicated audience of 30,000 within the Inside Curve community, Lane Bryant put in place the means for those members to share that information across their personal and public social networks, making it go viral. Lane Bryant's social media use in this particular instance truly highlights how when a brand creates an authentic and engaging social media personality then reaches out to listen to their customer base, momentous things can be accomplished together.

By addressing criticism targeting a particular TV spot within Lane Bryant's online community network, the reaction from brand loyalists, reporters, and the public defending and supporting Lane Bryant generated unprecedented press/media coverage across both traditional and non-traditional outlets including: TV, radio, newspaper and online/social media platforms.

"The Lingerie Commercial FOX and ABC Didn't Want Its Viewers to See" acquired the following online traffic totals during this time:

- **Over $40M in earned media on a $5M spend**

- **Ad shown on over 300 TV shows, hit over 3,000 blogs and online sites, including: Jay Leno, CNN, People.com, The Today Show, The O'Reilly Factor, The Huffington Post, etc.**

- **Effectively relaunched the Lane Bryant brand and introduced Cacique to the country, bringing in thousands of new customers**

- **2 million video views in three days**

- **Named the "Most Watched Ad in the World" by AdAge for two weeks in a row**

- **In AdAge's "Top Ten Most Watched Ads in the World" list for three weeks after that**

Quotes from the campaign:

"The upshot is that it was a fantastically orchestrated PR campaign."

- Michael Learmonth, AdAge Editor for digital media

"It created much more awareness than you would ever imagine for a television commercial."

- Thomas A. Filandro, Senior Consumer Analyst

"Possibly the biggest publicity campaign ever for a retailer."

- Omnicom

Case Study # 7: 21st Century Dental

Organization: 21st Century Dental; 21stCenturyDental.com

Background: 21st Century Dental is a dental practice and medical spa.

Business Need: Build relationships with their clients and soon-to-be clients.

Social Media Solution: Keep clients updated on Facebook by showing them new services and the hard-working/fun-loving staff; and reach prospects on Twitter with rare facts and lots of interaction (See page 111).

Business Result: Messages spread quickly about new services like the med spa and sleep treatments. Clients became more aware of services and expanded their purchasing power.

What actually happened:

With the help of Social Media Delivered, 21st Century Dental decided that the social media tools Facebook and Twitter would be best for their business needs. 21st Century Dental ensured that only select Facebook features were used in order to avoid presenting an overwhelming amount of information to their target audience. Clear, simple and uncluttered information allowed them to reach out proactively and increase their fan base. In particular, they selected the following Facebook features on Facebook.com/21stCenturyDental:

- **Video**: Allows user/brand to display product demonstrations, real-time customer testimonials, or other engaging content.

- **Photo Albums**: Feature a variety of perspectives about the brand to be displayed through images/pictures.

- **Active Wall**: Provides a forum where the brand is consistently followed up with a target audience and address comments/customer feedback.

- **Contests with Personality**: The crew at 21st Century Dental is a hard-working but fun-loving group. They showed this by having "Name that Tune" video contests on Facebook with a patient humming tunes while her teeth were whitened.

Facebook was only one element of the 21st Century Dental social media campaign. In order to reach out to their target audience quickly, the company opted to use Twitter as a catalyst for conversing with their current and future patients as well as the medical industry. Because Twitter offers various messaging options, 21st Century Dental could interact in different ways on Twitter.com/21CenturyDental:

- The background design was re-vamped to showcase an attractive design scheme using bold colors, with contact information being critical to recruiting followers.

- The company emphasized consistent replies on their Twitter feed.

They understand that interaction, not just broadcasting, is the key that has 21st Century Dental in Twitter's top-20 most-followed dentists in the world.

Case Study # 8:
Cable & Wireless Worldwide UK

Organization: Cable & Wireless Worldwide (Europe, Asia and U.S.); CWWorldwide.com

Background: One of the world's leading international communications companies specializing in providing critical communication network and services in the UK and globally.

Business Need: Persuade their clients' executives to buy into using social media to improve customer service.

Social Media Solution: A three-pronged approach across Facebook, Twitter and dedicated websites as customer service channels (See page 112).

Business Result: Measurable ROI both in terms of customer service and reduction in operational costs.

What actually happened:

In early 2009, a few of Cable & Wireless Worldwide's (CWW) clients raised the subject of social media. These clients were receiving service requests via social media. They wanted to understand how the marketing and communications activities they already had in place could be used to handle these requests.

As CWW dug deeper into the type of queries customers were raising regarding social media, they determined that it would be beneficial to explore the business model of using social media as a full-blown customer service tool.

There's a wealth of readily available information via social media that allows companies to gain real insight into their customers and improve the services they offer. For example, when customers were asked how likely they were to recommend the brand after resolving their customer service issues using social media, there was a 70% improvement compared to the same customer group being serviced via the telephone.

"Whenever the subject of social media is brought up, you will inevitably have objections," says Craig Palmer, Head of Customer Access and Contact Centres at CWW. "The key to overcoming those objections is by having a model that demonstrates tangible benefits."

Palmer's team found that persuading their clients' executives to buy into social media was a formidable challenge. However, says Palmer, "Once we were able to prove that there is an ROI on a social media-based customer service model, this became a much easier conversation." This was the first lesson CWW's team learned and one that is a common concern across all the businesses with whom CWW consults.

CWW's solution: defining a model that allows its clients to effectively implement social media as a customer service channel and measure the benefits. The model has three key tenets:

1. **Use a reactive listening approach**: Understand what your customers are saying and put rules in place to define how and when you intervene.

2. **Be a resource**: Monitor and act on trends. Post relevant, useful information that your customers will value, so that you will be regarded as a resource that the customer can trust.

3. **Combine proactive selling and customer service**: This is the area that offers the real long-term benefits to business.

By understanding these three areas and measuring the resulting improvements, Cable & Wireless Worldwide has modeled the ROI both in terms of customer service and reduced costs. Although CWW isn't likely to suggest turning off call center phones and using social media as a replacement, social media is redefining the business model of many organizations for the better and will continue to do so in the future.

Case Study # 9:
S.M.A.R.T. Restaurant Group

Organization: S.M.A.R.T. Restaurant Group, A Which Wich® Superior Sandwiches Franchisee

Background: S.M.A.R.T. Restaurant Group, is a Which Wich® Superior Sandwiches Franchisee that features 51 varieties of customizable, toasted "Wiches." The parent franchise now has over 100 locations in numerous states. This case study specifically features the Dallas/Fort Worth (DFW) locations.

Business Need: Target local customers within a national presence.

Social Media Solution: Twitter.com/WhichWichDFW and Facebook.com/WhichWichDFW (See page 113).

Business Result: Increased sales during promotion/special periods by using social media marketing.

What actually happened:

In addition to its delicious customizable sandwiches, Which Wich® Superior Sandwiches is also known for recognizing the technological needs of its customers, and thus certain restaurant franchises feature an online ordering system and numerous interactive benefits such as free Wi-Fi at several locations. So, it's not surprising that S.M.A.R.T. Restaurant Group became interested in how they could benefit their customers and themselves using social media. However, when you're part of a franchise, much of the social media conversation occurs at the national level, which caters to a wider audience.

Instead, S.M.A.R.T. Restaurant Group's Dallas/Ft. Worth Which Wich® locations wanted to regionalize their brand message, ensuring that their local consumers received tailored attention and conversation. With the help of Social Media Delivered, They decided that Houston and Dallas/Fort Worth focused Facebook and Twitter pages would allow them to realize these goals. Their efforts began with creating a set of vanity URLs for both the Facebook and Twitter accounts. Vanity URLS make a social media accounts more optimized and easier to find within the internet.

In this particular scenario, promoting these accounts within a franchise space was equally important. Shortly after the URLS had been secured, S.M.A.R.T. Restaurant Group President TJ Schier, in working along with the corporate office and the help of social media firm Social Media Delivered, also developed several in-store signage pieces displaying the URLs. This enabled these particular Which Wich® locations to capture store traffic attention and pieces displaying the URLs. This enabled these particular Which Wich® locations to capture store traffic attention and spread the social media message even further.

As a result of their social media efforts, these Which Wich® Twitter and Facebook accounts generated a connection with a specific target audience. Sales increased steadily as their content continued to provide engaging, educational, and interactive information. Plus, they made it very easy for their customers to find them online by expressing the exact website: Twitter.com/WhichWichDFW instead of saying "Find us on Twitter..." like so many brands make the mistake of doing.

On January 6, 2010, the S.M.A.R.T. Restaurant Group's Houston and Dallas/Ft. Worth Which Wich® locations held a 99-cent "Wich Day" and promoted it using their Twitter and Facebook sites. After the promotion ended, results showed that this location which had used Facebook and Twitter followers to promote this event achieved 30% more transactions at their location versus the other locations which did not leverage social media to spread the word about the promotion.

Chapter 3:
One Ball is Not Enough to Juggle

Have you ever watched a juggler engage a crowd by throwing around one ball? No? Of course you haven't. In the game of social media, many companies try just that. Unfortunately, when it comes to social media most people only think of **one thing at a time**.

Many companies decide the best way for social media to be handled is by their customer service department, either internally or outsourced. Other companies believe the right place for social media is the marketing department, where promotions and specials can be highlighted by a team of dedicated experts in their fields.

Right about now you're probably wondering which of the above I'm going to say is the "right" answer. Well, guess what?

The above are both correct in that you need to actively engage marketing and customer service departments to be successful with social media. However, that is just the tip of the iceberg. Social media is a ridiculously powerful tool and you need to be leveraging it for all parts of your company. Fortunately, that's just what this chapter is about.

What should you be using social media for? Here are a few areas of your company that can start leveraging social media today:

Customer Service

By definition, social media is based upon frequent interaction with important people, and the most important people in the life of your company are always your customers. They pay the bills and keep you fed. Nearly every comment or bit of feedback is a kernel of information to be exploited and explored, IF you treat it as such.

Make sure your customer service department is on the lookout for the following kernels of information:

- **Specific complaints about a new or existing product or service that need to be rectified immediately**

- **General grumblings that should be looked into further**

- **Rave reviews about a new product or service**

- **Trends people are mentioning that need to be followed up on.**

Many companies are getting better and better by speeding up response times and reducing costs for customer service departments through the use of social media vehicles such as Twitter or Facebook.

Some companies use social media to share the solution to a common product or service problem their customers experience so they can disseminate the information to large numbers of people quickly.

Contact centers are beginning to leverage the power of social media as well, and over the coming years I predict that you'll continue to see a rapid shift in the way contact centers and customer service centers leverage social media to solve complaints more rapidly and in front of the public eye.

When a company uses social media and publicly works to solve issues openly and honestly, they often develop "crusading customers." This is the term I like to use for the phenomenon of a company's own customers who begin to step in on behalf of the company via social media even before the company can respond.

The power of customers who will answer questions, right wrongs and defend you till the end, because they've seen your company earnestly try to do the same, is a very powerful weapon in your arsenal.

Social media is a great place to serve up customer service, but if it is the only thing a company does there, they are missing the boat.

What else should be included?

So glad you asked.

Marketing

We started out this section by stating your customers are the most important part of your organization, but to continue growing, you'll naturally need *more* new customers.

That is why marketing is the next important element to make sure you are growing through your use of social media. In this sense, I use marketing widely to include many things:

- **Advertising**

- **Branding**

- **Public Relations**

- **Specials**

- **Promotions**

- **Sales**

It confuses me when companies choose a PR house to handle their social media. I believe a good PR company is worth its weight in gold, but PR is only one aspect of social media.

So, find a good PR company and have them spread your message through social media, but don't ask PR to manage the advertising, customer service or other facets of your company that you should be addressing through social media.

Have your marketing department coordinate with PR to bring their ads, visuals and writing to life. For instance, if the marketing campaign is for a new line of skateboard designs, get with PR to see how they can translate your print, audio and video ads into flesh and blood.

Perhaps they can get some great press by having local skaters try out the boards "live" at the local skate park (with the popular media in attendance, of course).

Pump all of the content from marketing and PR through social media and take it further to real, everyday people. For instance, if you're debuting a new skateboard design, wouldn't it make sense to post videos of actual kids using the skateboard on YouTube.com to gauge the reaction? Here is a great way to have a two-sided conversation.

By posting these demonstration videos, you're saying, "Here's our new product – what do you think?"

By providing valuable feedback with their responses and comments, kids who view the videos are saying, "Here, let me tell you ..."

Now you are seeing how marketing and customer service begin to mix and work together through social media.

Company Goal Fulfillment

So, you've taken care of customer service (keeping current customers) and marketing (getting new customers). Now what?

Now it's time to leverage social media to take care of everything else or, more specifically, Company Goal Fulfillment. This refers to the items your company is working on that don't fall directly under marketing or customer service, and often includes items such as:

- **Recruitment**
- **Research and development**
- **Geographic or demographic areas of focus**
- **Business partnership development**
- **Acquisition and mergers**
- **Company funding**
- **Competitive research**
- **Social causes**
- **Employee recognition**

Many companies have no idea that social media can be used to assist them in doing inexpensive targeted research before the development of a new product or to promote the non-profit causes they support.

Many small businesses do not realize that, in fact, one of the best keys to finding investors for first-or-second-wave funding is through social media. It's a brave new world, my friends, and social media can provide you with ways to do business more efficiently and less expensively than ever before.

I recognize it can be challenging to think of something as supposedly "simple" as social media having so many possibilities, but doesn't everything in business touch on everything else?

Doesn't a slow-down in production affect shipping, delivery and customer service?

Doesn't a breakdown in hiring affect management and leadership?

Why should social media be any different? The main point to remember is that you shouldn't just say to each department, "Here, handle your social media and get back to me."

Social media works best when it all works in tandem. Bring your department heads together to discuss their goals and how they will use social media to achieve those goals.

Although I am seeing a clearer understanding rapidly evolve, I still hear some companies say they will just hire a few interns to take care of the social media. Because this technology is familiar to the younger crowd, it makes sense to have a young person in charge of it, right?

This is a common misconception. Although a younger person is more likely to be familiar with the technology and the tools, it is doubtful an average intern would bring the level of experience in marketing, customer service and communications necessary for representing the reputation of a company.

Putting an inexperienced person in charge of social media is like putting the phone repair guy in charge of your customer service calls. Just because someone knows the technology, doesn't mean they can oversee the goals of a strategic social media campaign.

Interns are valuable for their knowledge of the technology, but they should be led by a team that you would want representing your company in front of the press, in person or on the phone. After all, social media puts your company on display in front of the world.

Social media is where customer service, marketing and everything else about your company wants to accomplish should converge into one very public place for you to build relationships to get these things done.

Case Study # 10: The Women's Museum

Organization: The Women's Museum: An Institute for the Future

Background: A Smithsonian affiliate, The Women's Museum: An Institute for the Future, makes visible the unique, textured and diverse stories of American women. Using the latest technology and interactive media, the Museum's exhibits and programs expand our understanding of women's participation in shaping our nation's history and create a lively environment for dialogue and discovery. Thousands of stories recount public and private triumphs and the struggles of those who would be denied their freedoms in all its forms: political, social and spiritual. [Source: TheWomensMuseum.org]

Business Need: Maximize national exposure with a minimal budget, being a non-profit organization.

Social Media Solution: Twitter.com/TheWomensMuseum (See page 114).

Business Result: A rapidly growing national and international brand awareness.

What actually happened:

Even before you walk into The Women's Museum in Dallas, Texas, the indomitable beauty of its elegant art deco façade immediately overcomes you. When you enter the blissfully cool lobby and walk up the grand stairway, you pass the larger-than-life 'Wall of Words,' where a dozen quotes are presented from the most inspiring women in history – Susan B. Anthony, Eleanor Roosevelt, Mary McLeod Bethune.

Further exploration of the Museum yields the many stories of women that take place throughout U.S. history from 16th century to now, all presented in an awe-inducing venue that harnesses the power of interactive media. For example, users can watch videos of The Carol Burnett Show and listen to audio recordings of Aretha Franklin's four-octave voice.

Visitors can open drawers to discover hundreds of pop culture images in the 'Icons of Womanhood' section, or peruse the dynamic 'It's Amazing' section. This colorful, brightly lit glass labyrinth explores facts and fiction of past and present dealing with stereotypes and images.

For such a highly interactive and intricate multimedia experience to not garner a national audience would be a waste, and yet prior to 2008, that was precisely the situation facing the nine-year-old institution. "Here we were," says Lyn Scott, COO at The Women's Museum, "the only museum in the nation dedicated to American women's history, and yet we had no means of speaking to a national audience."

The mission of The Women's Museum was to "bring to life the voices, talents, achievements, aspirations and stories of the past, present and future;" to be appreciated on a national level. However, it faced the problems common to most non-profits.

Limited resources meant limited staff, especially for the marketing department, which consisted of one person. And like most non-profits, marketing had to make do with a slim advertising budget of virtually zero dollars.

"We were only able to justify buying ad space in smaller, regional magazines focusing on local tourism and rental events," says Haley Curry, Marketing Manager of The Women's Museum. Not surprisingly, this kind of geographically narrow focus provided limited exposure.

Prior to the advent of social media, the Museum's website was its only means of reaching a wider audience, yet it was still limited in its reach. Along came Twitter. Thanks to its ability to reach a wide audience and engage with fans from all over the U.S. and the world, the Museum quickly realized the potential of this new platform. "Twitter allowed us to make huge strides on a limited budget," says Curry.

Using only the highest-quality content that was a blend of both entertainment and information, the Museum was able to build a strong community of Twitter followers. Within the first year, The Women's Museum's social media outreach campaign was a huge success, attaining an impressive 12,000+ Twitter followers. Furthermore, @thewomensmuseum is ranked among the Top Museums on Twitter along with the Tate in London, MoMa and the Brooklyn Museum (*http:// www.museummarketing.co.uk/2009/06/09/top-museums-on-twitter/*) as well as being on the list of 20 of the *Top Nonprofits to Follow on Twitter.*

The most critical result of their efforts: About 60% of The Women's Museum's followers are located outside the Dallas/Fort Worth area, with 1% located internationally. The Women's Museum has achieved a strong presence and awareness, which continues to grow, not just nationally but internationally as well.

"Twitter also allows us to connect with our most enthusiastic fans and participate in a conversation that is constructive to our mission: create conversation and develop understanding of American women's history," says Curry.

That connection is critical for a museum with such interactive media exhibits that bridge the gap between location and thought. "Not everyone can visit The Women's Museum the building, but they can experience who we are daily at @thewomensmuseum."

Case Study # 11:
McDaniel Executive Recruiters

Organization: M.E.R. (McDaniel Executive Recruiters); JustCareers.com

Background: M.E.R. provides recruitment services for a variety of companies at the management level, for professional services, and for the outsourcing industry.

Business Need: To integrate the recruiting industry's fragmented social media presence into a single entity.

Social Media Solution: Create and develop a LinkedIn networking group dedicated to call center professionals (See page 115).

Business Result: As of 2009, the LinkedIn group has increased its membership to more than 17,000 and has become widely recognized within the industry.

What actually happened:

The recruiting industry is a large and diverse set of industry professionals whose main focus is to recruit talent and place these professionals in an appropriate company. In order to do this effectively, recruiting companies must ensure that their clients (the hiring company) are satisfied with the placements; customer satisfaction is evaluated using several different channels (i.e., email, web, phone, social media response, etc.).

The industry itself is a very active group with a dynamic need to communicate frequently for answers and solutions. Thus, the "networking" nature of this industry demands active management in regard to customer relationships.

In the past, call center professionals have also used blogs, websites and other social media tools to connect, network and manage their customers and handle related customer service issues. However, many of these tools were often fragmented, scattered and ineffective.

It was decided that LinkedIn, a powerful networking website, would be the ideal platform for unifying McDaniel Executive Recruiting with its customer base. During this time, LinkedIn was now host to a dynamically large "Call Center Professionals" group that would bring people together in a new dramatic way.

By recognizing this void, M.E.R. created a call center networking group on LinkedIn in 2008. Since its establishment, not only has it become the largest group of this type on LinkedIn for call center professionals (*http://www.linkedin.com/groups?home=&gid=71348*), but more importantly, it has enabled a large community of call center professionals to interact, socialize and help one another solve common business problems, bringing the community closer together through discussions about various customer response strategies. Today, this group has over 17,000 members and is well known throughout the industry.

"I believe our +10-year history of building and developing a 'global community' of CRM/BPO talent has positioned M.E.R. to recognize the power of social networking tools," says Chad McDaniel, President of M.E.R.

"Social media has made reaching out to this community much more efficient. Moreover, we've also been able to offer a 'return' for those involved by answering their questions, and inquiries with a relatively instant response and sharing of information."

Case Study # 12: The Adolphus Hotel

Organization: The Adolphus Hotel and its premier signature restaurant, The French Room

Background: The Adolphus is an award-winning luxury hotel with a golden reputation steeped in tradition in Dallas, Texas. Its premier signature restaurant, The French Room, is a 4-diamond restaurant renowned as offering one of the world's top dining experiences.

Business Need: Connect with devoted guests while exposing the unique personality of The Adolphus to younger generations unaware of the hip luxury that awaits them upon checking into The Adolphus Hotel and also while dining at The French Room.

Social Media Solution: Create a heightened online presence at Facebook.com/TheAdolphusHotel and Twitter.com/TheAdolphus via extremely diverse and highly interactive content focused on art, cuisine, travel, local history, pop culture and other finer things in life that appeal to the target audiences (See page 116).

Business Result: A passionate following of long time guests and people experiencing the property for the first time began connecting through shared discussion. The Adolphus became one of the most followed hotels on Twitter in the world. For the first time in years, The Adolphus saw a marked increase in new guests gracing the rooms of the hotel and the restaurant.

What actually happened:

David Davis, Director of Public Relations for The Adolphus for over 27 years, pours all of his talents into what is one of the most luxurious and loved hotels in the nation. When David approached Craig Scott, Managing Director, with his wishes to begin leveraging social media for the hotel, concerns arose. The Adolphus and The French Room both enjoy a highly respected, prominent reputation going back almost 100 years. Scott wanted to avoid alienating the hotel's discerning, international client base and risk sacrificing its solid reputation. Could this luxury brand maintain a refined image if it were present on social media platforms like Twitter and Facebook, which are typically associated with everyday wares, services, and brands?

The answer is a resounding yes!

With the help of Social Media Delivered as their social media consultants, David Davis and Craig Scott took The Adolphus down a path that few hotels – much less luxurious ones – had ever traveled before. Scott understood that in order to build relationships with new prospects, he would need to provide not just information but also a mix of entertainment and engaging content. Twitter.com/TheAdolphus serves as a platform to spread information not only about hotel happenings, but also for events happening around Dallas, allowing followers to be "in the know."

Thanks to Davis' long and rich tenure at the property, he enjoys relationships with incredible authors, artists, celebrities and executives both nationally and internationally. He wanted to be able to reach out to these contacts consistently in a light-hearted and entertaining way. The Facebook page allows him to do just that. Facebook.com/TheAdolphusHotel is like an online lifestyle magazine full of "bite" sized tidbits of entertaining, historical, informative content. This social media vehicle also enables The Adolphus to showcase the unique beauty of the property via photos and videos, allowing for immediate, direct interaction from its many fans.

The Adolphus Hotel Facebook Fan page also provides a unique business solution to an ongoing challenge – how to be competitive in a tough wedding market. For years, The Adolphus has hosted weddings of all sizes and all styles, but modern brides were spoiled for choice and were overlooking The Adolphus. But a Facebook initiative changed all that.

Each month, The Adolphus showcases a different wedding, displaying wedding photos for all to see and providing the newlyweds a bit of celebrity fame. The modern, sometimes edgy dresses juxtaposed against the hotel's historic beauty provide striking and unforgettable images. This initiative has helped position The Adolphus as a contemporary and hip locale for Dallas weddings.

The return on risk has been invaluable. The Adolphus's Twitter presence, representing the hotel and The French Room restaurant, has been responsible for generating an increase in brand recognition to a whole new, younger audience. The Adolphus is currently the #1 ranking hotel or restaurant in Dallas with over 7,000+ followers. It is also one of the most followed hotels in the world. The Adolphus now enjoys a revitalized reputation and has become one of the most sought-after wedding locations in Dallas thanks to its social media presence on Facebook.

The Adolphus and The French Room prove that there is a place for luxury through social media as long as you cater to the needs of the clientele in the way they wish to be engaged. The Adolphus has already been doing this in the real world since 1912 – the transition to social media was only natural.

Case Study # 13: Texas State Optical

Organization: Texas State Optical (TSO);
Twitter.com/TSONetwork; Facebook.com/TSONetwork

Background: TSO is a network of 120 doctor-owned-and-operated eye care practices in Texas, Louisiana, Arkansas and Oklahoma.

Business Need: Build and strengthen relationships with consumers AND with industry professionals.

Social Media Solution: Use Facebook as a platform for building relationships with their consumers, while using Twitter to connect and recruit professionals in the industry (See page 117).

Business Result: Established TSO as an industry thought leader; an increase in Facebook and Twitter following of 52% and 575% respectively, resulting in expanded brand awareness in the B2B and B2C arena.

What actually happened:

In early 2009, TSO, with the help of Social Media Delivered, decided that they could leverage social media to accomplish two primary objectives:

1) Build relationships with consumers to strengthen TSO's brand

2) Interact with industry professionals for the purpose of recruitment and developing relationships

TSO and Social Media Delivered decided that Facebook would be ideal for accomplishing the consumer-oriented objective, while Twitter would work well for the industry-oriented objective.

It was decided that the content to be posted on Facebook should be 60% educational, 30% informational and 10% advertising of products. This is an essential feature of social media usage by healthcare professionals: credibility is paramount.

The consumer must perceive the company or practice as a valuable information resource, unburdened by a profit-driven agenda. Hence, the percentage of content that refers to TSO products or services is intentionally minimized. The result of their efforts on Facebook was a 52% increase in fans in a three-month period, from 530 to 808 fans.

Moreover, TSO began reaching out to the optometry community via Twitter. Their technological efforts were considered mildly anomalous in the healthcare industry. Though there are many segments of the healthcare industry that are technologically advanced, the optometry profession is not usually one of those segments.

"A significant number of practices are not computerized, so what we were doing [on Twitter] was a bit unusual," says John D. Marvin, CEO of TSO. "Using Twitter was considered fairly progressive for our field."

Interestingly, TSO is less interested in seeking a return on investment and instead is driven to build communities. "Our goal is to inform our consumers and to be a thought leader in our industry," says Marvin. "Our endeavors on Twitter and Facebook do not stand alone; instead, they are integrated into a larger communications program, which includes attending conferences and trade shows, and generating industry publications."

For TSO, Twitter is merely the starting point to building a relationship with physicians and industry consultants. Additionally, Twitter elevates TSO's visibility in the community, thus creating further dialogue with their peers. Texas State Optical's efforts on Twitter resulted in a 575% increase in Twitter followers, from 130 to 877 followers in a three-month period.

Case Study # 14: General Motors

Organization: The General Motors Company; Twitter.com/GMBlogs; Facebook.com/GeneralMotors

Background: The General Motors Company, also known as GM, is a U.S.-based automaker with its headquarters in Detroit, Michigan. The company manufactures cars and trucks in 34 countries, has recently employed 244,500 people around the world, and sells and services vehicles in some 140 countries. [Source: Wikipedia.com]

Business Need: Following declaration of Chapter 11/363 Bankruptcy, General Motors needed to completely redefine its established brand image, which appeared to consumers as faceless, nameless, outdated and impenetrable. The new GM brand structure would require a more accessible and transparent feeling in order to help humanize the brand.

Social Media Solution: Build a diverse social media team, with CEO engagement and support, to handle all logistical/management social media operations, which allow the newly defined GM brand mentality of openness and engagement to be clearly communicated and fully accessible to the media, to the general public, and most importantly, to customers (See page 118).

Business Result: Held market share with four fewer brands, increased awareness and consideration, created solid customer loyalty and positive brand awareness.

What actually happened:

As the financial industry collapsed into decay in late 2007, things progressively worsened across all industries in America, including the automotive industry. A year later, corporate giants and small businesses alike continued to fear the worst was yet to come.

Despite countless efforts to prevent the inevitable bankruptcy filings, including "putting divisions and parts operations up for sale and cutting the size of its workforce repeatedly,"[*] problems continued to worsen.

On June 1, 2009, GM's worst nightmare became a reality when it filed for bankruptcy. Because of this drastic setback, and even with the U.S. government estimated to pledge an additional "$30 billion at least ... on top of the $20 billion handed to [GM] already," the future seemed uncertain for one of the Big Three American auto giants.

GM had weathered many difficult financial climates throughout its long history. In an article for *Business Week* reviewing General Motor's current financial state, reporter Ed Wallace makes a key observation: "[Even] after the 1910

---

[*] http://www.msnbc.msn.com/id/30389457/ns/business-autos/

@mariashapiro30 @mariashriver @MariaSimone @MariaSmiling @mariatchijov @MariaVistage @maricarmenmar @Marie_Ang @marie_claire_au @marie_elg @marie_remedies @MarieBenard @MarieDenee @marieespiritu @marieeved @marieforleo @MarieLasVegas @marielle722 @MarielleL @marigoy @Marii_xxx_ @marijevh @MariJoHarding @Marikablog @MarikoHulme @mariliaborges @marilyn_messik @marilynbohn @MarilynTDowning @marinadimandis @Marinds @MarineTechMike @marinic @Mario_Marketer @MarioAlcaraz @mariobox @mariocabrera @MarioKaestner @Mariop72 @mariorodriguez @mariosolanoSEO @maris_life @MarisaCorser @marisacp51 @MariSmith @marisoldiaz @marisolmaribell @Marissa_J @Marissa_stone @maritune @MariusOna @mariusz123 @Mark_Campanale @mark_charlotte @mark_crase @mark_earle @mark_ellam @mark_fallows @mark_koenig @Mark_Sheldon @mark_tetzner @Mark_Vaudreuil @mark_warner @mark33 @MarkAllenOnline @markanastasi1 @MarkAPatten @MarkARodriguez @MarkBakerEvents @markbaxterdc @markbel3 @MarkBilton @markbnorwich @MarkBowser @MarkBrimm @markcahill @MarkClayson @markclement @markcolless @markcreaser @MarkCWinters @markdanshaw @MarkDavidGerson @markdgibson @MarkDimension @Markedia @Markedon28 @MarkEricJohnson @Markerter @Market_Articles @market_expert @market_talk @MarketBistro @MarketeersCLUB @Marketer_Guide @marketer_jobs @Marketer_UK @marketer22 @MarketerCalkins @MarketersShop @MarketFX @markethinks @MarkEThurston @marketing @Marketing_2015 @marketing_4_u @Marketing_Apes @marketing_biz77 @marketing_gal @Marketing360 @MarketingAlly @MarketingApes @MarketingArmada @MarketingBrian @MarketingBtrfly @marketingbus @marketingbykat @Marketingdonkey @MarketingDonut @MarketingEpsert @marketingfem @MarketingFool @marketingsrl @marketingisus @MarketingJedi @MarketingKnoHow @marketingldr @MarketingMav @MarketingMikeR @MarketingMobi @MarketingMoma @MarketingMud @MarketingMuscle @MarketingProfs @MarketingPulse @marketingseo2 @marketingstatic @MarketingStrtgy @marketingsurfer @MarketingTipsGR @marketingtwitts @marketingwa @marketingyudai

Financial Panic ended, rising sales proved that GM was viable in any condition."

Over the decades since its founding in 1908, the company has persevered through the good times and bad. But more importantly, the GM brand has built a name for itself to represent "for almost a century a symbol of American industrial might"*. In a word, GM's brand has proven to be resilient.

Yet consumer confidence had plummeted and the company needed a fresh approach in order to restore faith in its heritage brand. Because of its consistently solid market share and size, GM had a big opportunity to proactively rebound from this destructive period and rebuild a lost relationship with its customers. It did so with social media.

In May 2009, GM put together an extended social media team consisting of members with backgrounds in finance, media relations and marketing. Their task: implement and oversee a tidal wave of social media touch points that introduced the freshly restructured GM brand mentality with openness and consumers at the center.

First, using platforms like Twitter and Facebook, GM's social media team listened carefully to what was being said about its brand and acted quickly to rectify misconceptions about the company. For example, Mary Henige, Director

*http://www.msnbc.msn.com/id/31354374/

of Social Media & Digital Communications for GM, saw a comment on Twitter from a customer who wanted GM to stop closing down smaller dealers and instead to "shut down their company-owned dealerships."

Within seconds, a member of the team responded to that customer explaining that at GM, actually there are no "company-owned dealerships." In reality, all dealerships are independent, often family-owned businesses passed down through generations.

Although this example illustrates only one customer's incorrect perception, it's highly likely that many others probably thought similarly, which impacts GM's brand negatively. However, when GM used a social media vehicle like Twitter to publicly and positively respond to the misconception, they were able to correct the negative comment proactively and without distancing the customer.

The era of social media makes handling this type of communication with a customer more possible than ever before. Communicating and listening intently to a customer is ALSO one of the most important things a business should be doing at all times. This is just one of many examples of how GM was able to set the record straight by communicating directly with customers and prospects via social media.

Next, GM created an unprecedented program giving the

public direct access to the CEO via social media. GM's CEO at the time, Fritz Henderson, understood the importance and necessity of active listening, being open and engaging with consumers. Through a series of live web events, customers, the media, and the general public were encouraged to participate in Q & A sessions and press conferences with Henderson.

The ability to speak one-on-one with the CEO of a major corporation like GM seemed almost too good to be true, and in fact, some assumed it was just a PR "hoax." However, staff recorded Henderson typing his answers during a web chat using Flip Cam technology in order to prove his active participation and to thank GM supporters. The video coverage was posted on GM's Facebook page as well as on vehicles, and was quickly disseminated across the social web.

An "Ask Fritz" forum was also created whereby customers could exchange ideas and information with the CEO. Within six months, over 16,500 customer comments and questions were addressed. GM managed not only to "wow" its customers with this campaign, but it set a new standard of engagement, demonstrating its values of openness and transparency, building consumer confidence and deepening customer loyalty.

Additionally, GM launched an interactive website, GMReinvention.com, inviting visitors to "Take a look at the new GM." The site provides a wealth of informative videos about GM and its vehicles, as well as opportunities to chat, get industry news and get to know members of the organization. Since June 2009, the site has generated an impressive 1.5 million unique video views and 1.6 million unique web visits.

By being honest, direct and real with customers, GM has been able to regain the consumer respect and loyalty that it had lost. What's more, a whole new breed of GM "brand ambassadors" has emerged.

These enthusiastic customers create buzz around GM products via their social networks, helping GM build its business. Additionally, these "brand ambassadors" often go to great lengths to defend the brand in the face of negativity or to correct misinformation that may be circulating about GM.

These conversations are taking place in real time in the social media space, which means they are reaching an audience of hundreds if not thousands. And the message is that much more powerful and credible coming from a peer rather than from a GM representative.

In this age of social media and the aftermath of the

recession, corporations more than ever before are held to a higher standard of ethics, professionalism and transparency. It's becoming harder to bury flaws because social media serves to magnify them. Instead of running away from social media, General Motors embraced the new technology and seized the opportunity to reinvent its outdated brand.

Thanks to GM's savvy use of social media, results have been steady market share, brand awareness and customer loyalty. While there's still more work to be done, this iconic American brand sees a bright future as it continues to reinvent itself through the power of social media.

Illustrations

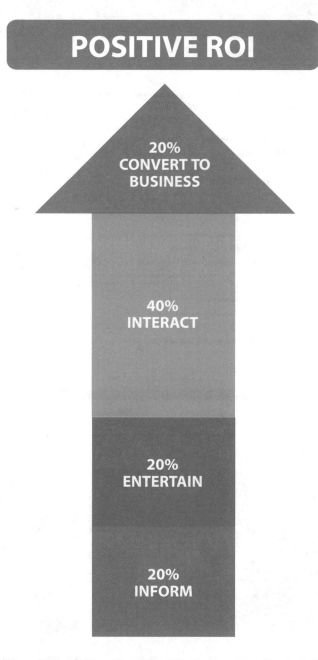

THE SOCIAL MEDIA EQUATION™

MAYO CLINIC
Center for Social Media

HOME   ABOUT   BLOG   EVENTS   NETWORK   NEWS   SERVICES ▾

NEWS

Below are links to news articles and blog posts about the Mayo Clinic Center for Social Media:

July 2010

- Minneapolis *Star Tribune*: *Mayo Clinic to open social media center* – 7/27/2010
- KAAL-TV: *Mayo Turning to More Social Media* – 7/27/2010
- Rochester *Post-Bulletin*: *Mayo Clinic create Center for Social Media* – 7/27/10
- 33 Charts: *Mayo Clinic Center for Social Media: What it Represents* – 7/27/2010
- MedCity News: *Mayo Clinic looks to train other hospitals in social-media use* – 7/27/2010
- KTTC-TV: *Mayo Clinic creates Center for Social Media* – 7/27/2010
- I Crashed The Web: *Mayo Clinic launches a Center for Social Media* – 7/27/2010
- *Wall Street Journal*: *Health Blog Q & A – Mayo Clinic's New Center for Social Media* – 7/28/2010
- Kaiser Health News: *Mayo Leaps Into Social Media Marketing* – 7/28/2010
- Conversation Agent: *Leading an Industry: Mayo Clinic Rolls out Center for Social Media* – 7/28/2010
- Fierce Healthcare: *Mayo Clinic aims to accelerate online presence with new social media center* – 7/28/2010
- CNN Health: The Chart – *Mayo Clinic starts social media center* – 7/29/2010
- iHealthBeat: *Mayo Clinic Launches Center To Help Groups Adopt Social Media* – 7/29/2010
- Twin Cities Public Television: *Almanac* – 7/30/2010
- PSFK – *Mayo Clinic Announces Healthcare's First Center for Social Media* – 7/30/2010

August 2010

- Scien
- AHD
- Neu
- 8/2/20

Search

CATEGORIES

Select Category

ARCHIVES

Select Month

RECENT POSTS

Help Wanted

Friday *Faux Pas*

The Importance of Being Nimble (Part 2)

Legal Issues (Part 4): Specific Suggestions When Drafting Your Policies

It's All About The Patient!

Legal Issues (Part 3): General Thoughts on Developing Your Social Media Policy

Viral video, internal communication-style

LINKS

Mayo Clinic

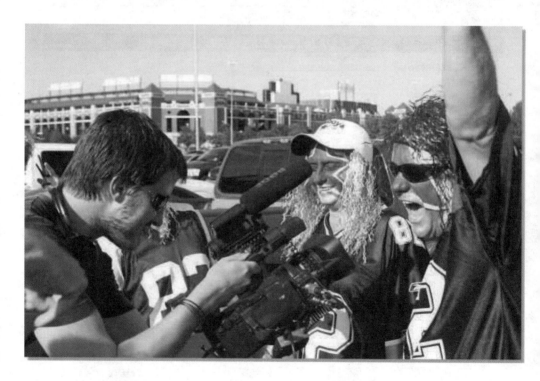

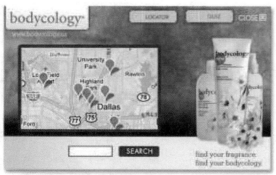

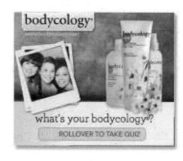

Linked **in**   Home   **Profile**   Contacts   Groups   Jobs   Inbox (7)   More...

Edit My Profile | **View My Profile**

Eve Mayer Orsburn (you)

CEO Social Media Delivered, Author of Social Media for the CEO, Social Media Speaker, Social Media Pro, @LinkedinQueen

Dallas/Fort Worth Area | Marketing and Advertising

Eve Mayer Orsburn Speaking to a group of Vistage CEO's at the Park Cities Club this morning then heading to the DART Women Owned Business Summit with my team to display my company.

1 day ago · Like · Comment (2) · See all activity

Current	• **CEO | Social Media Strategies | Social Media Sites | Social Media Content | Social Media Speaker** at **Social Media Delivered**
Past	• VP | Social Media Strategies | Social Media Sites | Social Media Content | Social Media Speaker at Steinbrecher and Associates • Dir | Social Media Strategies | Social Media Sites | Social Media Content | Social Media Speaker at AIGB • VP Sales | Social Media Strategies | Social Media Sites | Social Media Speaker | Web 2.0 at TM Century see all...
Education	• Louisiana State University
Recommendations	**33 people have recommended Eve**
Connections	**500+ connections**
Websites	• SocialMediaDelivered.com • Join My Linkedin Group
Twitter	• LinkedInQueen • SocialMediaDel
Public Profile	http://www.linkedin.com/in/evemayerorsburn

twitter

21CenturyDental

Name 21stCentury Dental
Location Las Colinas Irving
Dallas TX
Web http://www.21stCe.
Bio Spa Dentistry & Med Spa
in Las Colinas, TX creating
gorgeous teeth, skin,&
improving patient health
through better sleep. We
have a Dentist for you in
DFW.

3,546   3,467   62

Tweets   1,949

Favorites

Actions
block 21CenturyDental
report for spam

You both follow

Following

View all

More like 21CenturyDental

Follow
Followed by @DesignerDepot and @LinkedInQueen

**Check out what our patients have
to say about our service, staff and
facility: http://ow.ly/2dFYx**
35 minutes ago via API

Tired of seeing those tiny little spider veins in your legs, or
around your nose? Call us, we can help you take care of that.
about 17 hours ago via API

Radiesse—As seen in the Oprah magazine...and we carry it
here at 21st Century Med Spa!
about 18 hours ago via API

Enhance your beautiful smile, with beautiful skin!
about 20 hours ago via API

According to the American Academy of Dermatology, acne
affects 40–50 million Americans, making it the most
common skin disease in the US
about 21 hours ago via API

Thank you for following: @krishnapatil100 @sallyshealth
about 22 hours ago via HootSuite

facebook

Search

21st Century Dental   Like

Wall   Info   Photos   Twitter   Links

Add to My Page's Favorites
Suggest to Friends

"Vision, Experience,
Compassion...Expect Everything"

Information

Location:
4301 N MacArthur Blvd
Irving, TX, 75038

Phone:
972-255-3712

Mon – Thurs
7:00 am – 5:30 pm

Fri
8:00 am – 4:00 pm

516 People Like This

21st Century Dental In 1816, one of Sir Isaac Newton's teeth was sold for
$3,633. When converted to today's currency, that is $35,700.

July 23 at 10:34am · Share

21st Century Dental At 21st we take care of your whole body, that's why
we've got a Medical Spa. We do tightening, facials, laser hair removal,
botox ans skin rejuvenation to name a few.
http://www.21stcenturydental.com/21stCenturyMedicalSpa.htm

21stCenturyMedicalSpa
www.21stcenturydental.com
Sedation and Cosmetic Dentistry in Irving Las Colinas / Dallas / Ft. Worth;
Veneers, bleaching, lumineers and Invisalign; treating headaches, snoring
and sleep apnea.

July 22 at 11:13am · Share · Report

WHEN AND WHERE

Date: Thursday 13th May 2010

Time: 5:00 PM – 6:30 PM BST

REGISTRATION

To register all you need to do is click on the link below – it only takes a couple of minutes.

>> REGISTER NOW <<

AGENDA

Join us for this complimentary webinar and listen to respected international industry speakers who have embraced a social media response strategy talk about:

- What worked, what did not work?
- If they did it again, how they would do it differently?
- What did their customers have to say about it?
- Did social media increase or reduce customer service costs?
- Can social media generate new revenue?

SOCIAL MEDIA – HOW WILL YOUR CONTACT CENTRE BE AFFECTED?

If you ask for one of the biggest buzz words or phrases heard today you are likely to hear a resounding chorus – "SOCIAL MEDIA!"

Brands are about reputation and response. However, social media has created an environment where companies no longer control their own brand.

Everyone is talking about it, but let me share with you four pressing questions:

1. What is driving customer response to social media?

2. Do Contact Centres represent a viable channel to drive a response to social media?

Some companies have actively embraced monitoring of their brand across social media; however many have not implemented a customer response and strategy to proactively engage social media circles...

3. What needs to happen next?

If you think your customer response will not be affected, think again. Social media has opened a whole new paradigm to customer behaviour and how that affects your brand and your company's customer response reputation.

4. Is your contact centre ready?

WHO'S INVITED

The webinar is designed to be a "do not miss" for all companies embracing social media response. We are welcoming a large international audience who will be joining our speakers from England, the United States and Canada.

twitter

Home Profile Find People Settings Help Sign out

TheWomensMuseum

Mark your calendar for a special celebration Aug 25th, the 90th Anniversary of the 19th Amendment at The Women's Museum: http://ow.ly/2iTwR
about 16 hours ago via API

ninotchkab @TheWomensMuseum me. just better. :)
about 16 hours ago via web in reply to TheWomensMuseum
Retweeted by TheWomensMuseum

CenturyofAction An historian RT @TheWomensMuseum What do you want to be when you grow up?
about 17 hours ago via web
Retweeted by TheWomensMuseum

bardic_lady Director of Dramaturgy at OSF. RT @TheWomensMuseum: What do you want to be when you grow up?
about 17 hours ago via web
Retweeted by TheWomensMuseum

Jeanette Rankin of Montana, elected in 1916, was the first female member of the U.S. House of Representatives.
August 25, 2010 11:00:21 PM CDT via API

We love telling stories through exhibits about women who overcame obstacles to reach their dreams.
August 25, 2010 10:31:10 AM CDT via API

Did you know the Dreams of Flight exhibits features two pioneers from Texas? Bessie Coleman & Jeana Yeager, who hailed from Ft Worth.
August 25, 2010 8:57:42 AM CDT via API

Lyndalowa Author Sara Paretsky and her "get off the pot" feminist attitude RT @TheWomensMuseum Name 1 woman who has been an inspiration to you.
3:26 PM Aug 24th via web
Retweeted by TheWomensMuseum

etacar11 @TheWomensMuseum How about a group of women? The Harvard computers: http://tinyurl.com/crywkm
1:35 PM Aug 24th via web in reply to TheWomensMuseum
Retweeted by TheWomensMuseum

volume_ctrl Lina Bo Bardi @architectmag No designers or architects named yet ... RT @TheWomensMuseum Name one woman who has been an inspiration to you
1:13 PM Aug 24th via Tweetie in reply to architectmag
Retweeted by TheWomensMuseum

cdrobot @TheWomensMuseum Lise Anne Couture of Asymptote Architecture is an inspiring female architect. http://ow.ly/2uo3k
3:52 PM Aug 24th via Hootsuite
Retweeted by TheWomensMuseum and 1 other

Name The Women's Museum
Location Dallas, TX
Web http://www.thewo...
Bio Women's history museum highlighting heroines stories & interesting tidbits of information for all types of women.

18,131	18,081	1,204
Following	Followers	Listed

Tweets   4,076

Favorites

Actions
block TheWomensMuseum
report for spam

You both follow

Following

View all

More like
TheWomensMuseum

The Women's Museum:
An Institute for the Future

The Basics
National women's history museum
Smithsonian Affiliate
Located in Fair Park in Dallas, TX

Homepage
www.thewomensmuseum.org

Blog
thewomensmuseum.blogspot.com

Photos
flickr.com/thewomensmuseum

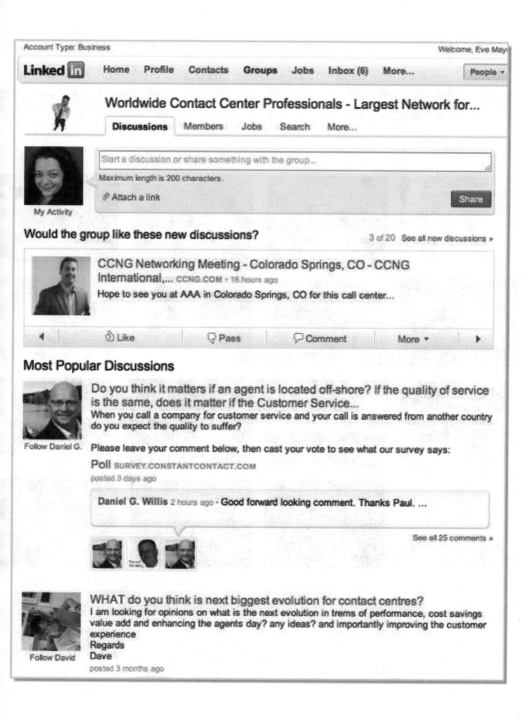

facebook Search

Autumn's Bridal Portraits at The Adolphus
By Adolphus Hotel · View Photos

👍 Like

Location

The Adolphus Hotel, Dallas, Texas

Autumn's bridal portraits at the historic Adolphus Hotel – the "Palace on the Prairie" – located in the heart of downtown Dallas, Texas. Images by Lynn Michelle Photography – we shoot fabulous people.

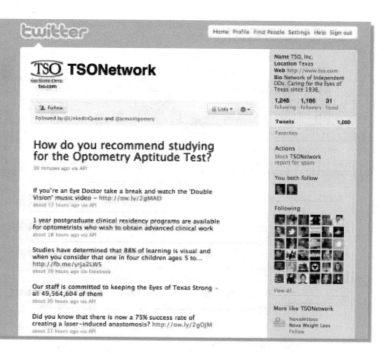

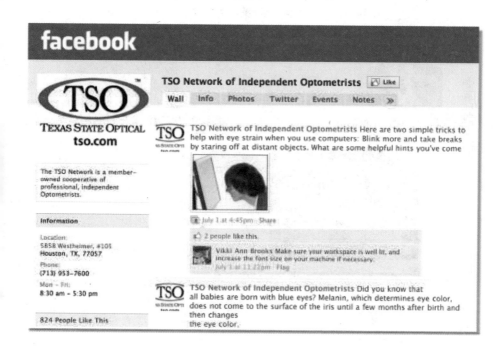

Re: conversations

Re: Buick and GMC
08/31/09, 12:30pm EST
Hosted by:
Susan Docherty
Join Chat

Re: OnStar
09/08/09, 10:00am EST
Hosted by:
OnStar Leadership
Join Chat

Join us for live scheduled chat sessions where the people helping to reinvent GM answer your questions about our progress. Get started by clicking "Join Chat." If it is in progress, you can sign in immediately. If it's a future session, you can sign up to receive a reminder.

>> See a full list of upcoming chats

Can't attend the chat session live?
See what was discussed in our archive.

>>View all transcripts

Chat

TELL FRITZ

Share your ideas, thoughts and suggestions directly with GM CEO Fritz Henderson.
He'll read them and respond to as many as possible each week.

(255 maximum character limit)

Enter Your Comment Here

>>View Responses   >>Continue

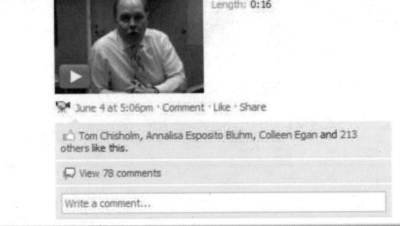

General Motors GM CEO Fritz Henderson finishes up his live webchat on Thursday June 4, 2009 and Thanks Facebook Fans in a quick video!

Jun 4, 2009 5:06pm
Length: 0:16

June 4 at 5:06pm · Comment · Like · Share

Tom Chisholm, Annalisa Esposito Bluhm, Colleen Egan and 213 others like this.

View 78 comments

Write a comment...

Chapter 4:
The Social Media Equation™

If this book were a hamburger, this chapter would be the "beef."

So if you pay attention to nothing else, remember this because I'm about to tell you what no one else is willing to spell out. Exactly what is the magic formula to have social media convert to business?

Let's say that, in addition to being a great business person, you also happen to be a great friend. One of your closest friends is a woman named Julie. You and Julie enjoy spending time together at concerts, networking events and with each other's families. You've known Julie for years and the friendship you share is a joy.

One weekend Julie calls you and asks for your help. She's calling you to see if you can help her move some heavy item, let's say a sofa, from one floor to the next early on Sunday morning.

You really love Julie, but Sunday is the one morning of the week you sleep late and you're really not that "friendly" before your morning cup of coffee. However, you set your alarm for 6 a.m., dutifully head over to Julie's house, and carry the heavy sofa up the stairs without complaint.

The question is: why?

The reason, in this case, is evident: **Julie is a great friend**.

In fact, 80% of the time you're with Julie, the friendship is rewarding, fulfilling and fun. So, because of the rewarding 80%, the 20% of the time when Julie asks for help – be it moving the sofa or listening to problems at work – you're always there for her. She's earned that much.

Such is the essence of a personal relationship for most people: as long as the majority of it is positively rewarding and affirmative, then the 20% of "work" you have to put into it is well worth the time. Of course, there are periods when those numbers may fluctuate, but those would be happy relationship numbers for many of us.

This is how I want you to treat social media for your business. After all, social media is simply enabling you to speed up the rate at which you **build relationships**. No longer do you have to attend 5,000 networking events to reach 50,000 people. (In our case, 50,000 people all over the world.)

You should still attend those networking events, but you can reach just as many people in a fraction of the time using social media. And relationships, as we all know, will translate into business, that is, profits, when nurtured correctly.

The fact is, if you're asking people to do things for you, such as visit your restaurant, come to your store, order online, use your service, or buy your product, you need to make it worth their while.

At least 80% of the time it has to be rewarding for them to come to your blog, watch your videos or read/listen to what you have to say. If so, then they'll naturally and willingly come "move your couch" or rather, buy your stuff, when/if you ask them.

The Social Media Equation™ – 100% Effective

The problem for most people isn't necessarily presenting a good product or service to the world. The trick becomes finding the right blend of social media content to help you communicate effectively and have that communication convert into business growth.

Not to fear! Through years of serving clients from hospitality to hospitals, I've created what I call the Social Media Equation™ to help you address exactly what you need to do to make your social media efforts more effective. This equation takes the guesswork out of what you are doing by giving you a precise methodology to follow.

Through our work with clients from various countries and industries we discovered this: assuming you are using the correct social media vehicle for your business goal, the recipe for success is basically the same. This is not surprising to me. I know through experience that if I am working with a quality product or service, then sales methodologies and customer service methodologies work the same, regardless of the industry.

So, what IS the Social Media Equation™? Simply put, to achieve a positive ROI, you need to express yourself on social media using the following types and percentages of content:

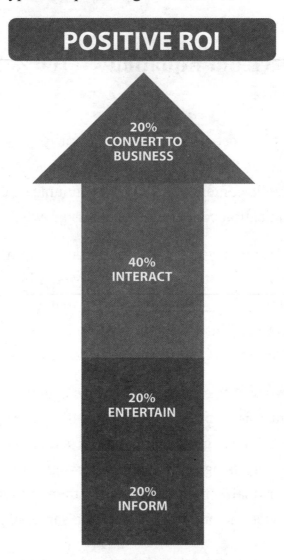

POSITIVE ROI

20% CONVERT TO BUSINESS

40% INTERACT

20% ENTERTAIN

20% INFORM

THE SOCIAL MEDIA EQUATION™

- **Informing - 20%**

- **Entertaining - 20%**

- **Interacting - 40%**

- **Converting to business - 20%**

This equation of informing (20%) + entertaining (20%) + interacting (40%) + converting to business (20%) equals (=) a Positive ROI if done seriously, consistently and energetically.

If you remember nothing else in this book, remember this equation.

We've worked with businesses and people all over the world, from restaurants to dentists to CEOs to nurseries, plus everything and everyone in between. The reason this equation works so well is because it applies to just about every business, every time.

If you can inform, entertain and interact in the right amounts (which adds up to 80% of the time) then you can spend the last 20% of your time doing what we all came here for: convert to business.

Now that you know the Social Media Equation™, let's break it down by category:

Informing - 20%

The very first step when communicating through social media is to inform.

As enjoyable as the internet is, very few of us sit down at our desks with a focused plan to waste a few hours surfing online. Typically, we sit down and get onto the internet to learn something, fix something, scratch some itch or fill some need.

A friend is contemplating plastic surgery, so he gets on the internet to research local doctors. I'm thinking about planting a garden, but don't have a clue how to begin, so I look for tips online. My daughter just started soccer and needs some new cleats, so I shop online because I'll get the answers I need in lightning speed.

That doesn't mean I'm not going to go to a shoe store with her and buy them in person, but I want to be prepared so I go online first. In other words, we are coming to you for some kind of information, so don't let us down!

As with any relationship, you have to start with giving. With social media, you are giving your connections information they are seeking, and it can come in any form, such as video, writing, etc.

Whatever form it takes, the information should come in specific, valuable nuggets people can use right away, such as facts, statistics, steps, tips, answers, etc. It should be information your organization has that others want.

So, for instance, if you're a garden center, you can offer tips about the best cuttings to plant for the upcoming growing season. If you're a plastic surgeon, post a short video of one of your patients asking you typical questions and you providing answers.

We have found that the best amount of the social media marketing mix is to **inform 20% of the time**. The information portion of the equation serves as a "teaser" and a way to showcase special knowledge that your organization has.

You can also serve as an aggregator of information that you know your audience wants or enjoys, and put it all in one little neat place for them. This information does not necessarily need to have been created by your organization.

For example, if you are a doctor but you find a helpful blog on WebMD.com, you might choose to comment and repost this blog because you know it will be of particular interest to your patients. In these cases, you would always remember to give credit and link back to the originating source of information.

Another important point with the 20% informing is to remain consistent. If you are an airline, include airplanes and other related subjects such as fuel, travel restrictions, packing tips, top destinations, hotel reviews, attraction information or safety requirements in your information.

Include subjects you know will be enjoyed by your prospect and client base. For example, if your airline caters to business travelers who fly to Asia, you could provide information about doing business in Asia or on customs that should be honored.

As tempting as it is to be creative (see next part of the equation), don't throw in information about random unrelated topics. For example, if you are an airline, don't give information on gardening tools because the audience may get confused. They are there specifically for information about airplanes, topics related to travel, or topics specific to that group, not gardening tools. By straying too far from the expected topics, you risk alienating your audience, which may cause the members to walk away from the relationship.

Entertaining - 20%

Think back to the last really superb speaker you had the pleasure to see present in person. Surely this person was speaking on a topic that interested you and she no doubt supplied you with the information you desired when you agreed to attend. But, what made the speaker outstanding?

Usually, a speaker can keep the attention of her audience because she not only informs, she entertains! An excellent speaker will hold an audience in the palm of her hand and keep it there. A speaker can make you laugh or cry, but most importantly, she is entertaining enough so

@Muzachan @mvassistant @MvdVeen @mverver @mvkumarvijay @MVP_SEO @mvpombogdi @mwarnersmith @MWCAshley @mwerner022 @MWGEnt @mwpatrick @MWreckazRadio @mwrenelt @mwsmedia @MWYT @Mx7Goldrush @MxNCinema @my_advice @My_Blog_Review @my_dog_ate_it @my_gold @my5pillars @myaaachoo @myadventureguy @myairwaves @MyAirZero @myalli @MyAlt @MyAppleStuff @MyAtlantaFord @MyBabyBeds @mybarefootbliss @MYBELARUS @MyBestCasino @mybestnews @MyBidShack @mybigcrazyworld @MYBLASTCAPBIZ @myblogusa @myBoboBags @myBoost @MyBrainEnhancer @MYBRAINSELLS @mybrandz @MyCaricature @mycents_today @MyChatToText @MyckeyFinns @MyCollegeOnline @MyColorCopies @mycontent @mycorporatmedia @mycraigslister @MyCultivus @MydaddySaid @mydailydues @mydailywine @mydala @Mydancepro @mydesignpod @MyDFWMommy @mydietchef @myDigitalGadget @MyDiningSpot @mydogjerry @MyEbisu @myen @MyEntredex @MyEventGuru @myfashionqueen @myfirsthome @myfirstrobot @MyFitCoach @myfpm @MyFreelancePaul @myfreshberry @myfriendniro @MyGamingworldUK @mygetaClue @mygiftsecrets @mygirlcass @MyGizmoRocks @mygreencard @myhandmadegifts @myharleynews @MyHarvestUSA @myhrjobsearch @MyHubTV @myihotels @MYIL1 @MyIPhonics @MyJobScope @mykieoyler @MyKuteKid @mylender @MyleneDuffy @Myler_ZZP @mylesbristowe @mylifebydesign @MyLiquorCabinet @MyLogoSource @MyLondonGuide @mylovepoetry @mylv8 @mymaktabaty @mymarketingnews @mymentortools @mymiaomiao @MyMillionaire @myMonstera @mymoxxor2009 @mymt @myMuse @mymxm @mynameiskimy @MyndersGlover @myneurotica @MyNewMediaIdeas @MyNextRehab @myniftynappy @myob247 @MYOBTrainer @MyOLCEA @MyOngobee @mypaintedthings @myPause_app @mypeopledb @MyPerfectGift @mypersonalvalet @MyPMExpert @mypoliticalopin @mypoliticscdn @mypowerfulmind @MyPRGuide @MyPrivateBank @myprofiler @mypulsecity @mypure @mypusaka @MyReincarnation @MyRFC @myrollingstocks @MyRonNoeLive @MyrtleBeachSEO @MySacredEnergy @mysalesrep @mysemicondaily @MySexHealthTips @MySexification @mysheernaturals that you actually **want to hear what she has to say**.

Social media affords your organization a very large audience and if informing is how you *get* people there, entertaining is how you *keep* people there. And the best way to do this is by "entertaining" your audience 20% of the time.

How do you entertain them? With things like anecdotes, obscure facts, engaging statistics, little-known histories, funny videos and shocking photos. The goal here is to provide amusement, the same way you might at a cocktail party.

Once again, it is important to reiterate that these gems of entertainment should always be related to your organization or to subjects that specifically interest your customers and prospects.

For example, if you are creating content for your social media campaign and you are in the dairy industry, you might post a link to a story about an artist making a sculpture out of cheese, complete with a picture.

Reusing great content in social media is allowed and encouraged as long as the information is readily available online and you are giving credit where credit is due.

Here are some other ways you can be entertaining around your social media efforts:

- **Use humor – the fastest way to create interest**

- **Post quirky, related news that applies to your industry**

- **Share video, audio or photos that are historic or strange**

- **Use a play on words**

- **Use little-known facts, people or imaginary characters**

- **Create characters from employees, customers or objects (e.g., create a character or icon to represent an employee, such as "Judy" from customer service)**

By all means, make them smile, make them laugh, "wow" them! However, do so in a manner that mirrors the tone and voice of the organization.

For example, when it comes to entertaining, an artsy ad agency will likely have a much edgier social media voice than a prominent hospital. But even high-end, serious organizations and brands can and should be entertaining. Moreover, they *need* to be entertaining 20% of the time if they are to achieve positive ROI with social media.

We have found this to be the correct percentage across the board regardless of industry. If you get the audience there with information and you keep it there by entertaining its members, then we get to what people go to social media for in the first place – to communicate and connect with others. We refer to that in our equation as Interacting.

Interacting - 40%

The most important thing to remember about social media is that it is simply **communication using new technology**. The ability to interact and communicate is the only thing differentiating social media from all other types of media that have come before it.

Most books on social media are about the technology, such as a video upload webcast or the vehicles such as Twitter or Facebook that you'll use in social media. The challenge of social media is not that the technology is so hard to master, it's that so few of us have mastered the art of communication. And it really is an art.

I keep going back to it, but this new development is so revolutionary it's vital you see it for what it is. Imagine being able to talk back to the ads in your magazine, or on your TV or car radio.

Imagine being able to conduct an online focus group every day, all day. Imagine an open customer service line 24/7 at every cubicle, and you'll get just a glimpse of what social media can be if you treat it like communication and not just another broadcast blast.

This is why I can tell you with certainty that social media is *not* a fad and will not go away **because humans will always be driven to communicate**. Social media is the new backyard fence, where one can gossip, pray, cry, laugh and share reviews about what's great, good, bad or neutral.

This need for communication is why you should be spending most of your time **interacting**. Interacting is the point where social media becomes a dialogue, where one-on-one engagement starts to turn relationships into business.

This is why I want you to spend the largest chunk of your time interacting. 40% of your organization's time using social media should be spent on interacting, which includes listening, questioning and responding. This, in sum, is communicating.

If you are trying to get to know someone at a party, how do you find out about them, what they like, and what they don't like? Do you do all the talking or do you ask and let them respond? In an ideal two-way conversation, you are sharing and exchanging.

It's called a dialogue, and it's exactly the same with social media! If you are spending your time doing all the talking, you don't provide any opportunities for interaction, which can be pretty boring for the other person, and may cause them to walk away.

Remember the young man at the Starbucks who blabbed on and on and then said he enjoyed talking "with" us? Well, I didn't get a chance to talk or ask questions and certainly can't say I enjoyed it.

It's the same in social media.

Here are some examples of encouraging interaction:

- **Example 1:** *Use a polling feature (available on several social media vehicles) to survey your audience members on their likes and dislikes of a certain product.*

- **Example 2:** *Pick a topic that is not about your product but is of great interest to your customers, such as a hotel talking about packing tips. Ask your "fans" to send in their very best suggestions, be it in video, audio or words.*

- **Example 3:** *Ask a multiple choice question. Let's say you are in the recruiting business and you ask, "What is the Most Important Quality You Want in Your Next Hire? Loyalty? Hard Work? Brilliance? Etc."*

- **Example 4:** *Ask a controversial – note I said controversial, not offensive – question. For example: There has long been a strong debate around the McRib Sandwich being a permanent item on the McDonald's menu or a recurring one. McDonald's bringing up this topic via social media would stir up lots of conversation.*

The list above includes a few great ways to encourage your connections to interact with you, but here is the most important part of interacting: **Listen to people online and respond**.

Listen earnestly and respond honestly. Yes, there are times when someone will be inappropriate or vulgar and it is best not to respond. I am also not suggesting that you respond to absolutely every post.

I *am* saying that you should truly listen to what your people are saying,

@nj_hbusiness @njchesney @njdevmgr @NJeatsNOW @njection @njfamilymag @njmotocross @njmovingguy @njobst @njones1920 @NJonesH @njunemployed @nkarnas @nkinnefick @NKYJennifer @nlbctim @NLCotter @NLCSocialMedia @nlinton @nlpconnections @nlplearn @NMACCommunity @NMandelaBay @NMbiz @nmcandle @NMFFFFD9 @nmfourwheeler @NMSNetwork @NMTAutism @nmyniche @NNChick @NnennaReviews @No_More_Day_Job @No1ForexGuru @Noa_Adamsky @NoahMallin @noahrinkle @NoahsArkClub @NoamKrig @noberg @Noblein @NoBullBroker @nocojobseeker @nocoparalegal @NoCoRentals @nocovoip @NocturnalAnimal @NoDebtU @noelbellen @noellebydesign @NoFadFitness @NogaYinon @nogueiradiana @NogueraNeill @NOH8Campaign @nohairsports @nohemorrhoids @NoHoBikes @nola_freebird @NOLAforFREE @nolah2o @NolanBailey @nolannaidoo @NolaOut @nolies4me @NoLimitsAsia @nolimitsforme @nologymedia @NoloLaw @nomadicnotes @NomadsLand @nomee @nomorebrains @nomorecellbills @nomoredayjob @NoMoreDedicated @Noname_Face @NONchan15 @NONchan51 @Nongling @noninvasive1 @NonPC_Cartoons @NookyLiverpool @NoosaCrest @NopalJuice @NoPanicAttack @NoPickles @NoPlateaus @noralmt @Norbert_Kloiber @norbertorlewicz @nordy389 @NoResultNoFee @norm_noordin @normah1 @NormanFrenk @NormRiceRealtor @norrisebooks @norskealbum @northernstocks @NorthstarAV @nortonsoft @nosalesneeded @nosmoking6days @NoStinkinBadges @Nostradamus36 @Nostringslovin @not_beige @notanadfeed @NotAProBlog @NotEasyToForget @NoteQueen @NotesOnDesign @NoTieIn @notjustagranny @notmarcocollins @NotNowNigel @notoriousGIG @NouveauGeek @novamir @NovaScotiahomes @NovaWtloss @NoVegans @NovotelMoscow @novowriting @novrealty @novronturkey @nowdiningfine @NowDiningVeggy @NowDiningWine @nowen56 @NowHiringJobs @NowIsTimeForYou @Nowplaying_4u @NowYouBeYou @NPI_purchasing @NPSocialMedia @NRGtheory @nrli @NSDFrisco @nsharp506 @NSHconsulting @nshn @nsikub @nstargs @nsteen @nsyteinc @NTebbey @NTJ @ntrofounders @ntxcopperheads @nubeerja10 @nubeerja3 @nubeerja5 @NucodeMedia @NuDigitalMedia @nudist_resorts @nudistclubhouse @NuErives and then respond as often as you can when a response or assistance is truly being asked for.

Oftentimes these interactions are taking place in the public eye, which gives you a great opportunity to address concerns, questions and even compliments, all in front of thousands of people/connections.

For example, your company may be totally unaware of an issue that the public has with one of your products. When a customer brings up that issue in the public eye (via message boards, on feedback forums, or on a blog), not only are you made aware of it, but you have the opportunity to discuss, brainstorm and solve this issue with others, while other connections are watching and taking note.

Even better, when possible, ask your online connections for suggestions in solving problems. Involving your online connections by asking them for help or ideas is a great way to build your relationship with them and make them feel that they are part of your brand.

By proactively solving customer issues in the public eye, you are establishing credibility and building confidence not just with that one customer, but with all the other customers and potential ones.

Many people think that the power of social media is to spread the message of the organization. While that *is* true, one of the lesser-known powers of social media is a direct line of feedback that reveals exactly what people are saying, thinking, and feeling about your product.

It is important to understand the message outside the four walls of your building, i.e., the customer perspective you wouldn't be able to hear so easily otherwise.

How often has your customer service department wished you could have heard a customer's phoned-in complaint? Or how many times have your salespeople tried to describe the passion in your customer's voice when he explained his excitement about the latest release?

Now a CEO or executive can be there virtually, and can hear it firsthand directly from the customer. That's why interaction is so vital to both you and your connections. It helps you gauge customer needs to know how to serve them better.

How long has it been since you listened to the music you play while customers are on hold? When was the last time you used a credit card to buy one of your products? When was the last time you shipped yourself a product and had to open it in a hurry?

Chances are, not very often. Well, your connections are on hold, using credit cards and opening your packages every single day. And they're often quite vocal on social media about these experiences.

For better or worse, interaction means they can actively tell you that the music you're playing while on hold is lame, scratchy or too loud. They can tell you that they clicked through six different screens to charge a $9.95 CD on your company web store; that's too many by far. They can also tell you how easy it was to open your packaging and how proud/happy they were that it was composed of 60%

recyclable materials.

I'm sure you'll agree that some, if not all, of the above information is critical to your future success. Interaction via social media is valuable for discovering your customers' tastes and preferences so that you can keep your customers happy.

If your customers are unhappy, they are likely to go somewhere else. If they are happy, they are more likely to stay in the relationship with you. Interaction can also result in new product ideas, improvements on current ones, and other valuable revenue-generating opportunities for your organization. For example, wouldn't it be amazing to display in public the fact that you are willing to listen to the good, the bad and the ugly and respond?

The Sheraton Fort Worth Hotel and Spa did just that. A guest, who enjoyed his stay immensely, wrote on Twitter to suggest that the hotel pool should not close at an early 10 p.m.

As Twitter is a social media vehicle open to the public, this message was accessible by anyone. Within 48 hours, the Sheraton Fort Worth Hotel and Spa thanked the gentleman for his comment and said that they would consider it.

Within the week, they responded publicly through Twitter and announced that the pool hours would be changed to close at midnight. They also publicly thanked the gentleman, by name, for his suggestion. Not only did the Sheraton Fort Worth Hotel and Spa respond to the needs of a valued guest in a timely fashion, they illustrated to the world that their guests truly are their priority.

When you engage customers directly to get their questions answered or their comments acknowledged, your company becomes something that is a living, breathing being to them. Through interaction, you are building a stronger relationship with your customers and your prospects. Remember to question, answer, listen and respond; in other words, the most amount of time interacting and do it 40% of the time.

Converting to Business - 20%

Imagine you've just walked into a networking event. And you're thrilled to see a stellar group of 300 CEOs, business owners and VPs. Well, naturally, you walk right up to the very first distinguished-looking gentleman you see. You can tell he's your type of client: nice suit, smile, handshake, the whole nine yards.

You shake his hand and say, "Hello, would you buy my stuff?"

What? Talk about rude!

I'm sure you can guess the outcome. He will likely make a kind excuse to visit with someone else at the event, and before you know it, he walks away and that's that. No second chances.

Believe it or not, when it comes to social media, lots of organizations act this way. They get onto a blog or a video or a podcast and all they do all day long is say, "Buy my stuff ... buy my stuff ... buy my stuff!"

They wouldn't dream of doing this in real life (or if they would, that's a whole other story!), so why do they think that just because they are using the tool of technology to communicate with people that it is okay to just sell, sell, sell?

Now, please don't misunderstand me. I am NOT saying DON'T ask for the business. You and I are both here for the same reason: creating relationships that ultimately convert to business. However, the example above is not the way to do it – in person or online.

On the other hand, there are a lot of companies that do a great job of informing and entertaining with social media. Some companies only interact, reposting and commenting on what people have already posted.

If you get into social media and you do a great job with interacting and talking to people but you never ask to convert to business, you get nowhere. Yet many social media experts think you should stop there. They shout to the rooftops that the purpose of social media is simply to build giving relationships, and that one should never sell.

I disagree.

Let's go back to Julie, your friend who needed your help moving her couch. Why did you so willingly move Julie's couch at 6 a.m. on a Sunday? Well, because she'd earned it.

She's a good friend and you know she'd do the same for you. This wasn't just some stranger; you had built a relationship based on trust and you knew that trust wasn't being squandered when she finally asked for help.

As is the case with any relationship, when you need help, **you ask for it**.

That's what I'm asking you to do with social media in general, and with the Social Media Equation™ in particular. A full 80% of the time I want you to **GIVE**. You give by informing, entertaining and interacting via your social media site/vehicle.

But 20% of the time, I want you to **TAKE** by asking for what you need.

What you need could be any number of things. It can be that your organization is looking for a new employee, business partner or investor. Maybe you need to collect information on a certain subject or to get people to participate in one of your company's events.

Maybe you want customers to read your blog. Maybe you have a need for a product or service and you want to know who you should buy from. And yes, converting to business may even mean asking people to buy your stuff.

It is okay to ask people to buy your stuff some of the time. After all, you are giving them valuable information, entertainment and interacting with them **80% of the time**.

Asking for what you need 20% of the time means both parties get something of value out of the relationship. And isn't that what relationships are all about?

The right way to convert online relationships to business is to actively treat these online communications and relationships in social media exactly like the ones you have in real life.

The right way to engage that distinguished CEO would be to walk up and introduce yourself. Say something like, "I'm Joe. I work with ABC Accounting." (This is **informing**.)

As the conversation progresses *naturally* during the event, you might tell a joke to lighten the mood, or offer a funny anecdote from the seminar. (This is **entertaining**.)

Next you might add something like, "What's *your* name? Tell me about *yourself*." (This is **interacting**.)

Then, at the end of the night after building a relationship and learning that there is, in fact, a need, you might ask for a lunch meeting for the following week. (This is **converting to business**.)

Now you know the secret to success with social media and how to make sure all this effort in the new world converts to business. Now go and use it and share your stories with me.

Chances are, I'm online right now.

Chapter 5:
The ROI of Social Media

So here it is, at long last, the million-dollar question – the question I hear from every CEO, CMO, VP or other **enter fancy title here** – "What is the ROI of social media? How does it pay off for me? What will I get out of it?"

In short, "What's in it for me?"

I'll be honest, I've left this chapter for last because it's the most difficult to explain and one of the most important concepts we must tackle. The truth is, because social media is such an evolving, rapidly morphing creature, no one can give a succinct answer on the return on investment it produces. There are just as many factors to measure as there are metrics to measure those factors.

Why, you ask? Because social media encompasses so many things that are typically measured in very different ways it can seem really complex to measure. And it may not be so easy to apply a "cookie cutter" approach to measurement from some of your other marketing and PR divisions.

For instance, there are excellent applications to monitor effectiveness in traditional print, TV, even online or radio advertising, but you cannot simply apply these to social media because social media includes elements of both broadcasting and communication. Advertising measurements are not designed to measure the value of interaction.

Some organizations that are heavily focused on leveraging social media to measure customer service may turn to customer service metrics (like net promoter scores) to apply a static form of measurement. However, since social media is a hybrid of marketing and communications, these measurements may not be accurate and will not always provide a clear picture of its effectiveness.

Even the most straightforward measurement of website traffic or online orders coming from social media vehicles will not tell the whole story, as many customers will spend hours on a company's social media vehicle interacting and, because of that influence, later go to your site to purchase a product.

Even though social media begins increasing brand awareness from the moment a connection first views it, ultimately, the customer often goes back at a later time to a different site or online location to purchase the product and thus, social media receives no direct credit for the sale.

That's the beauty, and the frustration, of social media. We know it's working for you, it's just hard to reach out and snatch a hard, fast measurement as you may be able to do in a postcard mailing, or a TV commercial blitz or even a new billboard ad campaign, for instance.

So now that I've told you all the reasons why it is difficult to accurately measure the return on investment for social media, now that I've brought you to the depths of despair thinking you'll never be able to measure all this hard work you've committed to, well, now I'm going to contradict myself and tell you **exactly how to do it**!

The Two Keys for Measuring ROI in Social Media

It's a bold statement to be sure, but it IS possible to measure the return on investment of social media IF you take two simple steps.

1.) **First, you need a specific goal**. What, exactly, do you want to achieve with social media? Specificity is key. You can't just say, "Well, I want to make lots of money." That's fine; so do I. But HOW do you want to increase profits? Be specific. Say something like, "I want to increase sales of a certain product or service by 25% using a concentrated focus on a specific social media vehicle (such as a blog, YouTube, LinkedIn, Twitter, Facebook, etc.) over the next six months." Now, *that's* a specific goal!

2.) **Second, you need a simple, safe and effective way to track the achievement of that goal**. This "tracking system," so to speak, will allow you to verify certain checkpoints along the path to achieving your goal at regular intervals, say, weekly, monthly, quarterly or annually.

By creating a regular series of goal posts and a trackable method of measuring achievement at each of them, you can now deduce the ROI of social media.

What I'm basically saying is that when you start with your latest, next or even your first social campaign, you must always start with a goal in mind *and* a plan on how you will measure that goal at a regular frequency.

Let's say there is a hotel – we'll call it the South Beach Bed and Breakfast – that wants to increase room bookings during the week to business travelers and has decided to use social media to achieve this goal. Regardless of the social media vehicle the South Beach B & B chooses to use, they must identify what's best for this task. More importantly, they must also decide how often they will measure the results before launching their latest social media campaign.

If the South Beach B & B is trying to lure weekday business customers, they will want to know fairly quickly whether or not their efforts are paying off.

Now, the folks at the South Beach B & B have clearly defined their goal for this social media campaign – to increase business during the work week with business travelers.

Next, they must figure out which vehicle(s) of social media their target audience is most likely to be using. Facebook or Twitter? LinkedIn or YouTube? Maybe they're on all four or one of the others that is best for

@PRSoapbox @PRspective @prstini @PRTGURU @PRTlovely @prtodd @PRTomShort @PRToTheTrade @PruComm @PrudenceCG @prumos @PRwise @psanjaymenon @PSAnney @PsicotecJobs @PSMOnlineRadio @psogge @PSonlineBiz @Psoriasis1 @pspinw @PSRegina @psusallc @pswalkofstars @PsychicHolly @PsychicLovers @PsychicRegistry @Psycho_Ex_Movie @PsychodudeCom @Psychogym @PsychoPuckLady @Psyqc @ptcyclist @PTGrouponHartfd @ptmartinez @PTNPokerSponsor @ptsaldari @pub44 @public_funds @public_image @PublicAnger @PublicDatabase @PublicGoodPR @PublicityGuru @PublicityHound @publicrelate @PublicSavings @publicwords @PubliGestion @PublishingGuru @publishover40 @PUBLISIDE @pubsterjosh @PuckGruenenwald @pueblocomputer @puffaddering @puffclean @pulido2010 @pullmarketer @pulse2dotcom @pulsedirect @pulsejfk @PumpkinPelfrey @punitastrologer @punkrockHR @puppetsholic @PurAman_Health @PurdueMensHoops @Pure_Hoodia @pure_ink @Pure_Truth @PureAveda @PureChuffed @PureDriven @puregroove_org @PureMagazineDFW @PuReMonKeY @PureNaturalDiva @PureshBeauty @PURIA_Spa @purplehayz @PurposeDirected @PurseDogTV @pursue_riches @Pursuitist @PushbackWines @pushboundaries @PushGapRadio @PushMeD @pushrealestate @PUSPEM_Found @putitinyourears @PuttingEdge_QC @PuttingEdgeBarr @puzzlepieced @pvesey @pvthotelschool @pweiderholm @pwilson @pwmcmahon @pwocken @Pyeman @PygmalionWeb @PYMConnect @PymeActiva @PYMLive @PYNcompany @pyracashbang @pyramidsonmars @pyxismultimate @pzadearmasq @Q_Consulting @q3technologies @qa4032 @qanetworkers @QD10 @QdME @QEDbaton @qfasttrack @QI_Business @QianaaRathburn @QiGong_Healer @QinaBrand @qlcoach @qofsevens @qoswhit @qpheVe @qqyuan @qstarweb @quadir386 @QuailHillEstate @QuakerQuotes @QualityHerbals @qualitylinks @Qualitytoys @QuaneshiaHolden @quaninte @QuantumAttract @QuantumKnight @quantumtouch @QuantumTouch_GS @quapet @Quaranj @QuarterJap @Quartz164 @Qubits_Toy @QueCEUs @QueenBeforTila @queenbuzzy @queenmarypat @queenmisha @QueenofJoy @QueenSchmooze @QueenTips @QuesaDYas @QuestarSoftware @quetzel2012 @Queue61 them. That's fine, but where are they most prevalent and which vehicle will they use?

Less Is (Really) More

I find companies to be most successful starting out using one social media vehicle at a time. This lets them really dominate that space and get comfortable with that medium.

So let's say that the South Beach B & B decides that Facebook is where they want to spend most of their time. They chose Facebook because it allows them to use graphics, post videos, and post at their discretion plus many of their guests have asked if they have a page on Facebook.

Now they begin using Facebook with the methodology we discussed in the **Social Media Equation**™, meaning they inform (20%), entertain (20%), interact (40%) and convert to business (20%).

Let's review South Beach B & B's goal: to increase weekday business traffic to their inn by a significant amount over the next three months. Now they need to track it. But how?

Well, for starters, they can monitor the traffic to their home page or (better still) to their reservation page directly from their Facebook page on a regular basis by using software such as Google analytics (which is free, by the way). This way, they will be able to determine whether or not there is an increase in the traffic to the reservations page.

A social media campaign is only as good as the content around which it is centered. Like any other successful marketing campaign, it will also require the correct frequency and the right audience.

In this case, the content South Beach B & B posts on their Facebook page must focus on their target and the goal. So if they're hoping for more business travelers, they would naturally talk about things that interest professionals, such as saving time on traveling for business, good business books to read on a two-hour flight, the best type of suitcase or laptop bag, stylish designs for business women, etc.

You Can't Measure It If You Don't Track It

Tracking is crucial to measuring the ROI of a successful social media campaign. South Beach B & B can track increased reservations **directly from their social media** efforts by offering specials or promotions that go to a specific landing page or use a specific code that is only tethered to one social media vehicle. Often companies use the same code on more than one social media vehicle, therefore diluting the effectiveness of their results.

For instance, South Beach B & B could offer a unique discount on their Facebook wall and mention a particular discount code, such as "FB123" when making their reservation.

This way, South Beach B & B would know exactly where those customers were coming from and would see that their social media efforts were paying off.

If South Beach B & B puts a specific code ("FB123") to a specific vehicle (Facebook), not only can they measure how effective their content and communications have been there, but they can also measure the hypothesis that their prospects they are reaching out to, truly frequent the vehicle AND act on those visits.

For example, if South Beach B & B is putting the same content mix and interactions on two separate vehicles such as Facebook and Twitter, and one is working and the other is not, then they may realize that there are not as many of their prospects on this specific vehicle and make adjustments accordingly.

The same kind of comparisons can be drawn by making the same offer on traditional media and on social media with different coupon codes or landing pages.

Many companies get so overwhelmed at the prospect of juggling dozens of social media vehicles and managing thousands of connections and writing, editing and posting (plus monitoring) tens of thousands of words of content that they never get out of the starting gate.

That's why, when starting out, I suggest that you only use **one vehicle at a time**. It may sound limiting at first, but starting with one vehicle at a time actually lets you focus all your efforts in one place to a.) get comfortable with that vehicle and, if you are just starting out, b.) get comfortable with social media in general.

So if Facebook pays off for our fictional B & B, great! They will need to keep up with Facebook on a daily basis but test other social media vehicles like Twitter and YouTube, etc. that may work as well.

Trust me, once you find success with social media you'll be addicted (like moi) and will be chomping at the bit to post more often on more vehicles mostly because you'll be experiencing a rapid spread of your message at a rate you have never seen before.

Parting Words about the ROI of Social Media

If your social media is difficult to measure, congratulations; that means you're doing something right. I'm not saying this is easy. I'm saying it can be done with the correct amount of planning and monitoring.

The fact is if you are truly interacting with your online network, it *will* be difficult to measure the ROI as a whole just as it is difficult for you to put a measurement of the ROI on the interaction your staff currently has with your clients and prospects.

What is the ROI measurement on the last visit a customer had at your retail store?

What is the ROI of the last PR event you did to promote your technology company?

It's not exactly crystal clear? Exactly!

Understand that social media is big – I mean REALLY big – and probably even bigger than all the buzz you may have noticed about it lately.

Why is it so big?

Social media is the culmination of marketing, customer service and communications in real time in front of everyone. Any tool that affords you to do so much and reach so many people for free cannot be summed up with one simple measurement. The power, reach, and effectiveness of social media are why you cannot ignore it.

You must embrace it now.

Conclusion
A Few Tough Questions

Question 1 – *Are all traditional forms of media going to wither and die because of social media?*

My background has been associated with media, marketing and ROI for a long time, so people have asked me if my passion for social media leads me to believe that traditional forms of media are no longer viable. Of course not!

Things are simply changing and you need to be part of that change because it is happening at a rate we have never seen before. I still believe in the power of television, radio, print and other traditional forms of media. In fact, I believe that people should get more mileage out of their television commercials that they have paid to produce beautifully by sharing them on YouTube.

Take whatever messages you are proud of in any format you have and recycle them. Squeeze every bit of juice out of them that you can. Someone may have missed that hilarious print ad which perfectly positions your product but then might come across it on their Facebook wall when their friend shares it and makes a funny comment.

Great content is great content, wherever it's found. Put that great content out there as often as you can in front of as many of the right prospects as you can.

Question 2 - *Is social media going to change the world and ruin it so humans don't even know how to communicate in person anymore?*

Yes and no.

Social Media is going to change the world and trust me, you can't stop it. It's too late and it's too fast. I do not believe it will ruin the world. It is changing the way we communicate and younger generations will have a tougher time with social skills in person because they will have less practice.

Humans are crafty and will adjust. Many people are concerned about the "evil downfalls" of social media because the tool is certainly a powerful one. However, like any tool, it can be used for good or evil.

The potential social media has to do good for the world astounds me. I am overwhelmed by the possibilities of rampant spreading of needed medical information, rapid warning abilities when inclement weather approaches an area, virtual mentorships to enable one human to help another with emotional support from across the world are just a few of the thoughts going through my head.

The truth is that social media won't change the world as much as it will put the world on display for everyone to see at every minute. It will amplify and magnify the good, the bad and the ugly.

So there you have it, **Social Media for the CEO: The Why and ROI of Social Media for the CEO of Today and Tomorrow.**

In this book we've covered the Why, the How and the ROI of Social Media. We have studied companies of all sizes sharing the truth about their business needs, challenges and ultimate success with social media. Now it is your turn to start your next, or first, social media campaign.

Remember, first and foremost, social media is a conversation; so the sooner you start talking – and listening – the sooner you'll build relationships that lead to business.

You cannot control social media, but you can influence it. And since somebody, somewhere is already talking about your company right now, the sooner you start influencing it, the better.

I challenge you to take a deep breath and leverage this tool to achieve that goal you've been salivating over. At first it will seem confusing and as if your company is bare for all to see. But, then you'll begin to see relationships forming.

What always has and always will build business between people are **relationships**. With social media, now, you can build those relationships more quickly.

Go for it!

Acknowledgements

Thank you to my mentors, David Schmidt, CEO of Schmidt and Stacy Consulting Engineers, Inc. (LinkedIn.com/in/DaveASchmidt); Lois Melbourne (Twitter.com/LoisMelbourne), CEO of Aquire; my mom, Regina Kojis Mayer; and my dad, Guy Mayer.

Thank you to my amazing staff who made serving our clients and creating the book simultaneously possible. Thank you to family, friends, associates, clients and more who helped us in many ways along the way. Thank you to the partners, clients and companies who shared their real life stories of social media success.

Thank you Rob Orsburn, Mia Orsburn, Laura Hale, Ruth Ferguson, Mary B. Adams, Amelia Clark, Amanda Montgomery, Angelo Benito Fernandez-Spadaro, Katy Mendolsohn, Justin Hess, Shilpa Nicodemus, Tom Jackson, Tony van Kessel, Del Wratten, Robin Kruk, Gavin Head, Bob Willems, Melissa Kovacevic, Jamie Nanquil, Alan Evans, Desiree Buckingham, Yvonne Riggs, Vicki Jasper, Schuyler Thompson and Petey the Gnome. Thank you to Angela Schmidt, Dave Schmidt, Paige Schmidt, Grant Schmidt, Jemimah Goodwin (Kermie), Degie Butler, Jiliane Faciane, Maria Martinez, Elizabeth Murdock, Joe Murdock, Amanda and Monty Montgomery for allowing me to finish my book at their beautiful lake house, my personal trainer in

@rpatwebb @RPIGroup @rpliska @RProject @rrhhol @rricart @rricker @RSACorp @RSALISTSERVICES @rsgbiz @RSHotel @rsjewell @RSMcGregor @rsmoot @rstbob @RSVPhere @rtaylor61 @rtbest @rtkrum @rtmjkwanbondcop @rtmoore77 @rtooms @rtstrategy @RTtips4u @rubbermaid @RubbermaidTwo @Rubee100 @RubenCurryBD @rubenq @ruby4love @rubyga49 @RubySlipperVA @rubywatch @RUcareers @Ruckdaschel2010 @rucsb @rude64 @rudezen @RudhirSharan @Rudi3CantFh52 @RudyCaceres @RudyFDF @rudys @Ruel_Antonio @Ruff_Ride @ruffinadvisory @RufRecords @ruhanirabin @RuiqiY @Ruivo @RulingCouncil @rumadison @runenthusiast @runlevelmedia @RunLove @runnerforchrist @running66miles @runningcouple @RunningPixel @RunSpired @rupertwhittam @rushabhrambhia @RushThePug @russ_dean @RussCoach @RussellOrganics @RussellORourke @russellquotes @russellshih @russian_rock @RussMack @rusty338 @rustybadge @rustyc77 @RustyCampbell @Ruth_Z @RuthBradford @ruthdfw @ruthhegarty @ruthless_phil94 @ruthmedia @ruthperryman @RuthSherman @ruv @rvandersar @RVLmakelaars @RVLuver @rvoegtli @RVRB @rvsbg @rwang0 @rwmovies @rwpcs @rwperkinsjr @rwphan @RWT711 @RWWRSS @rx4good @rxcareer @Ry_Curran @Ryan_Cornelius @Ryan_Dobbsy @ryan_gledhill @ryanbokros @ryanbovey @RyanCPeterson @RyanDehler @ryandeiss @RyanDerous @ryandmckinney @ryanleisure @RyanMakes @ryanmega @RyanPaine @ryanpinnick @RyanPrillman @RyanRancatore @RyanRobbins @RyanRockstarr @RyanSammy @ryansteinolfson @RyanStyleTM @RyanSuccess @RyanTheInvestor @RyanThompson @RyanV49er @RyanVistage @ryanyouens @ryanzuk @rycak @RyderMedia @ryersondmz @rytaran @s_adinugroho @s_ahsan @s_levaillant @S_NelsonBuckley @s_u_r_y_a_rockz @s_uccess @SOCIALCAPITAL @s2space @S4SRVTour @s6mkt4 @Sa_DiegoWeather @SaarMaxi @saaze @sabaidress @Sabaiweb @SAbestCPAs @SabineBraun @sabinelenz @SabineOsmanovic @sabita_anju @Sabrina_PHR @sabrinacoffin @sabrinagibson @sabrinasolesbee @SAbsalom @sacalvo @SacHarlows @sacrebleuwine @Sacredsecret @SacredSunbeam @sadhana8 @sadhanakh @SadieMHarris @sadodhifhhaihsh @SAdoreBoutique @sadoty @saedabuhmud @SafecountJenn

Dallas Angela Smith (Twitter.com/angiefit404), my CPA Wray Rives (Twitter.com/RivesCPA), and Lane Bryant for keeping me in style (Twitter.com/LaneBryant).

Thank you to Patty Farmer, Fred Campos, Dr. Kent Smith, Dr. Jeff Roy, Anthony Eggleston, John Biebighauser, James Wood, Amanda Williams, David Davis, Craig Scott, Jack Murray, Lee Aase, TJ Schier, Wanda Brice, Lyn Scott, Haley Curry, John D. Marvin, Chad McDaniel, Paul Chaston, Rick Harrison, Craig Palmer, Chris Yates, Shauna McLean Tompkins, Mollie Milligan, Brian Fabian, Matt Parvis, Betsey Brailer, Heather McGarry, Nick Charles, Donna Mclallen, Mary Henige, Jay Dunn, Joel Denver, Fleetwood Hicks, Kimberly Hutchison, David Boyett, Julia Danklef, Mary Hoffman, Michael Schwartz, and Rafael Pastor. Thank you to 21st Century Dental, Anheuser-Busch, Bodycology®, Cable & Wireless Worldwide, General Motors, James Wood Motors, Lane Bryant, McDaniel Executive Recruiting, Texas State Optical, The Adolphus, The French Room, Mayo Clinic, The Women's Museum, Which Wich, Boxcar Creative, Huddle Productions, Sheraton Fort Worth Hotel and Spa, and Shula's 347 Grill.

Thank you to St. Joseph, E.D. White Catholic High School and the Nicholls State University TAG program in Thibodaux, Louisiana for a great education. Thank you, Louisiana State University in Baton Rouge, Louisiana for having an excellent communications and business school. Thank you to the cities of Bunkie and Thibodaux, Louisiana, Irving and Dallas, Texas, and Paris, France for your kind support.

Special thanks go out to my Mom, Ms. Kovar (my first-grade teacher), Geppetto (my childhood dog) and Brod Bagert (an author) who are partially responsible for me becoming an author. When I was a child, Ms. Kovar, who was also my neighbor, lent me the book *If Only I Could Fly* by Brod Bagert. I was 10 and determined that I was brave enough to camp out all night in a tent in the backyard. Of course, I chickened out during the night and my mom tucked me safely into my bed. The next morning I discovered in horror that my Old English Sheepdog, Geppetto, had basically eaten the book and I was in big trouble! My mom, always knowing how to turn things into an opportunity to teach me important life lessons, told me I would need to do some chores to earn enough money to replace the book. This was back in the olden days before people had computers and my Mom couldn't find where to purchase the book. Somehow she tracked down the mailing address of the author. She had me write a letter to him explaining how my dog had eaten the book and asking how I could purchase a new book to replace it for my teacher. One night during dinner, there was a knock at the door and Brod Bagert had come to our house and brought me two autographed copies of the book – one for me and one as a replacement. Bagert told me how much he liked my letter, and that instead of paying for the books, I should repay him by turning this story into a book and sending it to him. He said that maybe one day I would be an author too. Later, he came and spoke to our entire elementary school. As a child, that event made a big impact on me and I'll never forget it. I have sent Brod Bagert the first copy of this book.

@sanjayakannath @SanjayCho @sanjodali @sanjoydalia @sanjuclicktweet @SanMarcoCoffee @Sanoviv @santaguitarsolo @Santana1969 @santidemierre @santilli @santosh0207 @sanuzis @sanyikaboyce @saodarafie @saoireobrien @SapereSolutions @sapiraaw @Sapphire_Dakini @SapphireBayCons @sapphiredrinks @saquinaakanni @SaraBeckford @SaraCrowe @SaraEyobHaile @sarah_4you @Sarah_Prentice @sarah_rahman @sarah_starry @Sarah_x_Rose @sarah_x10 @SaraHamil @SarahatDell @SarahAtPSBJ @SarahBuchanan1 @SarahButtonedUp @SarahCaminker @SarahCares4U2 @SarahEganMooney @SarahElles @sarahEmagee @SarahFulton @SarahGirl122 @Sarahhh91x @sarahkalaj @sarahkilbourne @Sarahlevy @SarahNelson_ @sarahnewton @sarahsantacroce @SarahStaar @sarahstips @SarahWhiteKC @sarahwitten @SaraJacksonValo @sarallenconsult @SaraLWood @SaraMazur @SaraMeaney @SaraSocialmedia @sarasotadream @sarelimarketing @sarinsuares @Sarita_Moreno @SaritaGandhi @sarjalis @Sarosresearch @SashaXarrian @sasikrishna @sass @SASSYKITKITTY @SassyNetworker @sassyword @satchmofest @sathishisaac @satori_zen @SatoriCoffee @SatoriNation @SatoshiSato @SatoyaJohnson @satpal192 @SatsugaiCat @SaturnSociety @saucyglo @Saul2884 @saulerick @saurabparakh @SAVAAHH @savageink @SavagelySocial @SavannahxLee @save_2_years @save4closureSD @savealifeparty @SaveDraft @SaveMeDebra @savenhawk @SaveOurPlant @SavetheDateing @Savetherehearts @SaveUrCredit @SaveYourCash @savingdinner @SavingEveryday @savingRXdollars @SavingsTKuljis @SavingYourMoney @SavorTheSuccess @savoysignal @savvybizowner @SavvyBoomers @savvyendeavor @SavvyExplorer @savvyinbiz @savvypromoter @savvysocialmed @SavvySpeculator @savvystudent @SavvyVA @SavvyWithJenna @savweightloss @Sawbuck @SaWht @SawyerTMS @SaxonHenry @sayiamgreen @SayingsOnLove @SaySocialMedia @sayvings @sazbean @SB_Entrepreneur @sba_daily @sbarton1220 @sbass10080 @sbblex @sbbuzz @SBCarmenSchmidt @sbeasla @SBellPR @sbenavid @SBGGlobalMobile @sbgraceLLc @sbilby @sblackburn @sboatella @sboulios @SBPacks @SBSConsultingF @SBToday @sburda @sburges2 @sbwalsh @SBweddings1 @SBWorkforce @sc72_ @Scabr

Author Bio:
Eve Mayer Orsburn

Ranked by Fast Company Magazine as one of 100 Most Influential People Online, Eve Mayer Orsburn is the CEO of Social Media Delivered, one of the largest social media optimization companies serving clients worldwide with consulting, training and outsourced social media needs. She has been featured by CNN Radio, CIO.com and speaks professionally to groups on the Social Media Equation™ which is her proven system for how organizations must engage in social media to generate a positive ROI. Eve also hosts the weekly radio show Social Media for the CEO. She shares social media knowledge that people can actually understand with an online network of over 50,000 fans, followers and connections every day.

You can follow or connect with Eve at the following links:

www.Linkedin.com/in/EveMayerOrsburn

www.Twitter.com/LinkedinQueen

www.SocialMediaDelivered.com

Press, interview and speaker requests should be submitted to her agent at press@socialmediadelivered.com.

Notes:

@SharleneStevens @sharlyn_lauby @sharmaineSainta @Sharon_Chan @Sharon_Higbee @Sharon_Phoenix @sharonarose @sharonbarel @SharonDexter @sharongadbois @SharonGaskin @SharonKnecht @SharonKolker @sharonmarkovsky @SharonMcP @sharonreinhard @sharpendtrain @SharronThornton @SharynAbbott @sharynread @shasherslife @shashib @ShatterboxVox @ShaunaCausey @shaunamclean @ShaunErk @ShaunHailes @shaunjamison @Shave_Dallas @shavereview @shawanyi @ShawHomesTulsa @Shawn_Leonard @ShawnaArmstrong @ShawnaCoronado @ShawnaCulp @shawnaseigel @shawnavercher @ShawnCMason @ShawnKCastille @shawnkhorassani @shawnmcpike @shawnrobinson @shawnrorick @shawnshahani @shawnweston @shaxx @shay2132 @shayr22 @shayzvia @shazelectronics @shcreations @SHDickson @SHDixon @ShearCreativity @shearerrima @SHEATHER703 @SheBlogsNetwork @shecky76 @sheelectric @SHEEmusic @sheenaindhul @SheetalJaitly @shegeek @SheidaMohebbi @SheilaAtwood @SheilaBerg @sheilacolon1 @sheilamba @SheilaStarkey @shelbilavender @shelbybowman8 @shelbyhomes @shelbylaneMD @sheldon1creates @shelhorowitz @shelitha4judge @ShelleyCall @ShelleyErnst @ShelliNoca @shellisxena @shelly_adams @shellybean123 @ShellyLodes @shellyroche @ShellyWolfe @SheltonCharl @Shelving_ @shelzolkewich @Shennee_Rutt @SheratonDallas @SheratonMoscow @SHerdegen @Sheree2055 @sheridansmithf @SheriGoddard @sherikayehoff @SheriLWatkins @sheriNOLA @SheriTingle @SherleyGrace @SherlindaNews @sherlyn99 @ShermanCSI @ShermanVisa @sherri_g @SherriGarrity @sherrilynne @sherrisheerr @sherroddine @sherry326 @Sherry9779 @sherryfetzer @sherryj @sherrykirksy @sherryroden @shersteve @sheryl_crawford @sherylmandel @shesaid_dallas @ShesSoSocial @SheTeamTweets @shetech @shibleylondon @shibuya246 @shiegie @ShiftAgeTrends @shilpanicodemus @shilpiarts @shimusicworld @ShiningClover @shinng @shionline @ShippersAgent @shiratoken @Shirestone @shiricki @shirlandc69 @ShirleMitchell @ShirleySchlag @shirleyshair @Shizo_Shirley @shizuka131 @shkebino01 @shmelanie @shobi23 @shockprices @ShoeBoxFiends @shoesdotcom @ShoestringGal @ShoesUK @ShoeTweeter @sholasmansion @sholist @Shon_Toni @shonajesta @ShoniquaShandai @Shookspeare @Shoosha @shopably @shopathome @shopexperts @ShopLOFT @shopmobbing @ShopOnlineNow88 @ShopperDolly @ShopperSaving @shopping_cheap @shopping_frenzy @shopping_ok @shoppingfocal @shoppingmobile @shoppologist @ShopSanctuary @ShopSaveBest @ShopSavvyMama @shopshareshine @shopsindex_com @shopwatchdeals @shore10 @ShoreFire @short_men @ShortcutsOnline @shortfilmfest @shortform_tv @SHORTME_EU @ShortNews_Auto @shortsalebabe @shortsalecourse @ShortSaleGuy1 @Shortsalejane @shortsalekid @shosized @shoutwit @showcaseclosets @showcasesuccess @ShowerThinker @Showingbook @showmetheodds @showmetheoddspr @ShowMoneyDotNet @ShowtymeJazzDuo @showupyourself @shreddel @Shreechirps @shresthayash @shreyam @shrinkingjeans @shu5kanou @shustir @ShutterBugGeek @shw72388 @Shyanneksom @ShylaGarder86 @ShylaKleppen86 @ShyneBeats @shynichols @Si_Clark @si1very @sibylleito @SicilianMentor @Sick_Tweets @SicolaMartin @Siddeley @Siddharth_IN @sidereelKendra @sidhai @sidneioliveira @sidneyeve @sidneyferresi @sidraqasim @SidWiseman @SIEGEINDUSTRIES @SierraSci @SiftGroups @Sifumusic @Sigbj0rn @sight2seize @SigisRam @SignatureAd @Signazon @signevent @signsnowdallas @sigsiu_net @sijj786 @silencespeaker @Silentium @SilentLeoinMTY @silgerd @Siliconhil @SiliconValleyDJ @SiliconVllyNews @SilkCharm @SilkRoad2010 @SillySticker @silverarcade @SilverbackCM @silvergreenssb @silverguru1 @silverimagelimo @silvermax2 @silveroaklimo @silverpeanut @SilverRaeFox @silversafecoin @Silversea @Silversmyth @silverzeal @SilviaOrtizNin @SilviaSchwibi @silviovailante @simanda @simasays @simchabe @simeonm @Simon_D_Young @simone_says @SimoneGuild @Simonephillips @simonevroom @SimonFord @simonfoster1 @simonhamer @simonkuo @Simonl33 @simonleung @simonmainwaring @simonpreacher @SimonRosenberg @simontoddcom @SimonWetherell @simonwhite @simple_heal @simple_truths @SimpleFit101 @SimpleHomeOrg @simplelb @SimpleMillion @simplemlm2 @SimpleNetSecure @simplestartcon @simplicityinc @simplybcreative @simplycast @simplygifts @SimplyGreenLife @simplyplates @Simpsonology @SimranSamtani @Sinareet @SinbadsSF @singlefathers @singlemomcoach @singlemomoftwin @sinith99 @sinkra @SinTecInc @SiODonovan @sipland @siqueiranathy @sir_gerold @siraf_2 @siraju @siremusicgroup @siriusbmusic @siriusdecisions @Sirjohn_writer @SirLinkedAlot @sirpokey @sirtwat @SirWebby @Sisdetec @SiSELpro @sisti @SitAndGoPro @SiteAHolics @sitemidas @sitepromotor @SiteSays @SitesDesign @SitewireAgency @sithburns @sixapart @Sixpaww @sixsevenx @Sixth_Sense_Mkt @siyyarah @SJackCreative @sjknutson @SJMMtogether @SJohnson85 @sjpheikkinen @sjsturkie @skalovers @skap5 @skarritt @skashliwal @skbrewer1 @SkeeterHansen @SkeeTVvp @sketchfanatic @SkiCoupons @skilletblack @skillscentral @SkillSource @SkillStorm @SkinCareDoc @SkinCareTweets @sking11 @SkinSpaMed @SKINTASTIC @Skintus @skip7547 @SkipAnderson @SKIPPROGRAM @SkipStein @skirtmuse @skittles_fanz @skquinn @Skretz @skump @skweon @SkyBlew @skydeer @skyebardallas @SkyeKing @SKYENICOLAS @SkyeYork @SkyHighFlyer1 @skyhithere @Skyito @skyjefans @SkylabGlobal @skylinemanager @SkynUK @SlabGA @Sladed @sladesundar @SlamStreet @slamtheworld @SlapApp @Slapman4u @SlavaRybalka @SlayterCreative @slcmyers @slcupcakes @sleepandsnoring @sleepbamboo @SleepSeller @slevaillant @SlideRocket @slideshare @slideshowguy @SLIDETVNEWS @slideworld @sliggitay @slimacaiformen @slimbeanscoffee @SlingshotERP @slkbrooke @slkeeth @sloaninnovation @SlopeViews @SlowCookerMate @Slowittedbanker @slump_diverted @slv35 @slvideo @Slycaj @slyfoot3 @SlyFoxOne @sm2extensions @SM3ND3Z @SmackPR @smaknews @smallbits @SmallBizBee @smallbizchat @smallbizIQ @SmallBizLady @SmallBizMuse @Smallcapalert @Smallcapweekly @smallcitymusic @Smalltalkwitht @Smart_Bride @Smart_Business @smartbandwidth @smartbarterusa @smartbloggerz @SmartBoyDesigns @SmartCookieMktg @SmartDad @SmarterSites @Smarthive @smarthomeguide @smartonlinetwit @SmartPropertiez @SmartStorming @smarttradepro @SmartVAforU @smartwebs @SmartWoman @SmartWomenClub @smartwomentrav @SmartyWireless @smaxbrown @SMBConsultant @smbirddog @SMCCoLUmBus @smcdallas @smcnulty @SMCSac @SMCVB @SMczarina @SMediaSource @Smehogolik @SMEMarketingTip @SMEPR @smerky216 @SMHappy @smichm @Smile_n_Shine @SmileBooks @smileegirl @SmilenErin @SmilesHappen @SMILEY_TOTE @smileyhealth @Smileysredbarn @SmilingMarketer @Smilinsteve @sMillys @smirchi @Smirnoff_There @smith_blarney @Smith_miniMBA2 @Smith_Tanya @SmithsonAnders @Smithy_001 @smitty_one_each @SMKSensei @SMM_UK @smm360 @smm41263 @SMMadagency @smmcamp @SMMmagazine @SMMonster @SMMProductions @SMMTweets @SMOBangalore @smoblogger @SMOCafe @SmokeClouds @SmokeyMiller @SmokingWomen @SmokinHotPR @smoochydate2 @smoothsale @SMOsocialmedia @smozee @SMP4you @SMSDallas @smt504 @smtrafficschool @SMU_HegiCareer @SMX_London @smykos @snackfanjapan @snagajob @snailmailnotes @snapon3 @SnapOutOfItShow @snappysalads @snbaird @sneakart @sneha_rg @Snikiddy @snipercatcher @SnippetGarden @SNKT @sno_buny @snorbrown @snowbird122 @snowboardcast @Snowbrrd @snowgator69 @Snowisle @SNReach @SNSanalytics @snstouch @snuckertook @snunitliss @Snuzzy @SO_pr @SoakUpLiving @soapboxdesign @SoapySoapy @SoaringCoach @sobreimoveis @sobseries @Soc_Media_Beast @soc08 @socalgirl @SoCalWriterGuy @soccer_football @SOCFX @sochristine @social_analysis @social_book @social_buttrfly @Social_Divas @Social_Dynamics @Social_Gal @Social_Manny @social_media @Social_Media__ @Social_MediaB2B @social_news @Social_Success @Social_USA @social2b @SocialBizTips @SocialBizWorld @SocialCashGuy @SocialChadder @SocialClassroom @socialcpr @SocialDave @SocialDojo @socialemon @socialexpertnow @socialfans @SocialFire @SocialFlyr @SocialGround @SocialGrow @SocialGuide @SocialInc @socialize4Money @SocializedWeb @socializeUAE @socialJacqui @socialjana @socialkaren @SociallySavvy4U @SociallySweet @SocialMarketin1 @SocialMassMktg @SocialMedia_Art @socialmedia_biz @socialmedia_mgr @Socialmedia_Mk @SocialMedia_NZ @SocialMedia_U @socialmedia283 @socialmedia2u @socialmedia4bus @socialmedia78 @socialmedia815 @socialmediabiz @SocialMediaBuch @SocialMediaBust @SocialMediaCRE @SocialMediaD @socialmediadeb @SocialMediaDel @SocialMediaDFW @socialmediadmd @SocialMediaEat @SocialMediaFan8 @SocialMediaGo @SocialMediaInEd @socialmediainmd @SocialMediaJew @SocialMediaJob_ @SocialMediaMax @SocialMediaMaze @socialmediamind @socialmediamn @SocialMediaMum @Socialmediapath @SOCIALMEDIAPRO1 @SocialMediaSol @SocialMediate @socialmediatek @SocialMediaWonk @SocialMktgDiva @SocialMktgMgrSF @socialmouths @SocialMPH @socialmrkting @SocialMtgExpert @SocialNapa @socialnate @socialnetandyou @SocialNetDaily @socialnetmarket @SocialNetNanny @SocialNetworkIt @SocialNetworkTV @SocialNetworkUs @socialnews09 @socialoomph @socialpage @SocialPMChick @SocialPotency @socialpr @SocialPRMarket @SocialPro @SocialPsyche @socialradius @socialram @SocialRockers @socialROI @SocialSammy @SocialSavvyGeek @SocialStylist @SocialSundayNL @socialtips @socialtoddler @SocialToolKit @socialtweeting @SocialVenture @SocialVisor @SocialWants @socialware @SocialWebMktg @socialwebnet @SOCIALWEBPR @socialwendypr @socialworkplace @socialxblog @SocietyBakery @sociotope @SOCJacki @socks2739 @Socks4HappyPPL @SOCLoriandMark @SocMandthePea @socme2 @socmed_superman @SocMediaBeach @socmediabrain @socmediaforum @SocMediaRckStr @SocMediaReviews @SocMediaTravel @SocMedRetweeter @socnetnews @socrecruitau @SOCSuccess @Soda_Hurts @Soffici @SofiaKeck @sofiazmf @sofiemoulin @SofitelDC @SofitelPhilly @SoFlaCommercial @SoFlaTechLawyer @soFNcute @SoFreysh @softapps @SoftBeddingSets @softinet @softsolution @softspotbywozzy @Softsquatch @software_forex @softwareblogger @SoftwareForFree @softwurkz @sogeshirts @SoGoEarn @SOGRnetwork @sohealthy4u @sohlfl @SOHLTC @SohlUSA @sohoaccessories @SOHOBusiness @SOHP_com @sokairavi @Sokos6 @sokule @sokule1 @Solamar @solar_power_kit @solardude1 @SolarEnergyNews @solarfeeds @SolarGurus @SolarIdeas @solarisdesigns @SolarisStudios @solarmoneysaver @solaroy @SolarPowerNow @solarpowerwell @SolarSecurity @SolaSalonStudio @SoldOnEbay @SolfegeRadio @solismarchela @SOLive_RBatzer @SollevaGroup @solofo @sologan @solomons_homes @solomonsucceeds @SolSolutions @SolTecElec @solution2peace @solution416 @SolutionCoach @Solutionman @Solutions4biz @SolutionsBoy @SolutionsDog @solutionsvault @SoluzioUff_2008 @solvate @somaJohn @SOMD_Waterfront @Some1Has2Sayit @SoMeCentral @SomeChum @somediaintegcon @Someguynamedpat @SomeLifeBlog @SomersetMtg @SoMEsg @somistvan @somodii @SONARconnects @SongMonkey5000 @Songpeople @SoniaHolland @sonicallstar @sonja4health @SonjaandLibrary @Sonny1974 @SonnyAhuja @SonnyDayDreamer @sonnyfe @sonnyg @SonnyJohns @Sonnymalek @SonnyTuesday @SonOfGoom @Sonos_DMU @SonyaDomanski @sonyaga @soocee @soorajmukh @SoothingSkin @SoovoxSocialIQ @SooWhoopcom @sooz100359 @SophieBifield @sophieheng @SophomoricTumor @SoravJain @sorenbreiting @sorensson @soriuq @sortprice @sos_haiti @soshle @SoSoJo @sosusereva @sotiris1 @SotomayorScotus @SoTravelNow @Souihli @soulbmx @soulcaretv @soulfoodnetwork @soulfulbeauty @SoulHeartPart @soulkisser @soulmagnet75 @soulpossum @soulspiritual @soumyapr @SoundbiteCoach @soundlifeed @soundtastykid3 @SouperSalad @souplantation @sourabhgoho @sourcer21 @SourcerKelly @Southeasternr @southeasttouris @Southern_Living @SouthernGifts @SouthernGirlDrm @southernskiesag @SouthlakeChiro1 @SouthWestFord @southwestliz @SouthwestMedia @sovbiz @Sovereign28 @soverland @SOWeiterbildung @SOXGUY @soxiflue @spaatwillowbend @SpaceSnark @SpaceyTracy2 @spamitis @SpammingReport @SpanishNow @SpankyBrown @SparBernstein @spark_pc @sparkie5150 @SparklicAcid @sparklife @sparklingonline @sparklingruby @sparklyscotty @sparkypowell @sparticatv @SPARTICUSIAN @spassas @Spbwealth @spdesigns1 @SpeakerNinja @SpeakerSharyn @speakersnetwork @speakingbadger @speakingexpert @Speakingroses @SpeakingTech @SPEAKMANENT @SpeakSay @SpecHosting @SpecialCupid @specialdesigns @specialmedia @Specisoft @Spectrumfcu @spectrumgraphix @SpeedCameraPOI @SpeedCoaching @speedhot @SpeedLearnNow @speedmarx @speedupyourlife @speljamr @SpencerHorn @SpencerMontgom @Spencersa @Spencerswife @spencerw3 @SpenceSmith @spes123 @SPFsocial @Spherion @sphoward @SpidermanGuru @spidersandmilk @SpiderWriters @Spiewak @Spike72AFA @spikehumer @SpilledInkRepU @spillspace @Spin_Thicket @spin1success @SpineBBMag @spinecor @Spinecor_brace @spininternet @spiraluptoday @spiritedal @SpiritEssences @Spiritfriends @spiritledrecov @spiritniche @SpiritOfAutism @SpiritualCarter @SpitCreekRanch @Splarr @splgroup @spmu @spohlit @spoilerSource @Sponsume @Spoonfulofchoco @spoortsdood @sporebuster1 @spornaso @sport1912 @SportConference @SportinaHotels @sportinggoods1 @sportnewsdude @Sports4398 @sportsbetcappin @sportsbetspro @SportsGuy @sportsosphere @SportSpotter @SportsPower @sportsviews @SportsZooRadio @Sportz1on1 @SpotOn3D @SpottedWombat @SpouseCentrals @SpreadingJam @Spredfast @SpringAqua @SpringfieldEdge @springfwd @SpringhouseEduc @SpringsSEO @sproutqueen @spryd @Spunky_PR @spurdave @spurinteractive @spwelch @SPwrite @SpychResearch @spyphoneguy @spyrosm @spyshopguy @sqltech2 @squaredcloud @SquareToesKern @SquawkMe @SqueezeItIn @squidoo_u_2 @Squinkman @sramana @srBurtonCook @srdill @sreede @srimudigere @SriniMetta @SrinivasNarne @srirams @srivanihyd @SRQRepublicans @Srschierling @SRStran @SRVP @ss_telecombum @ssaikia @sschwend @SSDTEAM @sseagal @ssentamu @ssilvestrone @SSInc_STL @SSMVlogs @ssossen @SSP080594 @Ssussanin @sswindale @ST_Louis_Rams @St0pSmokingNow @stablesolutions @staceysoleil @staceywalker @Staci32 @stacicavalcante @StaciDLA @StacieinAtlanta @StacieShepp @staciestaub @stacigauny @stacihtims @StaciPerry @stacy_laurence4 @stacycrosby @stacyharp @stacykinney @stacyknows @StacyMossHR @staenman @staffingsavvy @Staged_2_Design @stagingdiva @STALJO @Stalwartcom @StalyonMusic @stample @Stan_Lang @StandardofTrust @Standing_Stones @StandingFirmCM @StandOutMan @standupcomedy @StandUpComedy7 @stanfossum @StanGill @stangwizdak @StanHjerleid @Stanimiroff @StanLenssen @StanleyGale @stanleysuen @stanlouw @stansmith2 @stantonmjones @Star9905 @Staralicious @Starbucker @starchycarb123 @starctchr @starfishclinic @starkcb @StarlightAff @starstreet @StarStruk @StartABizRite @startaheart @StarTargets @StartAtOne @StartNewBiz @startupacademy @startupbiztalk @startupcoach @StartupGuru @StartupKey @startupprincess @StartupPro @StartUpsCA @STARTUPSMAP

@startwithmoxie @StarwoodBuzz @StateInsurance1 @StateIman @statesman @statu_boy @status_il @StaybridgeDFWN @stayclassyCHI @StayPutFishing @StayTunedReport
@stayyoungernow @StBartsPremium @stbonaventure @stbsmith @STCSTREET @StealingKitty @SteamRollerEQ @steamrollerinc @steamykitchen @steelemodels
@Stef_Cormont @Stefan_Berg @Stefan_Fischer @stefana127 @stefanbell @stefaneyram @stefanholt @Stefanie_Bauer @stefantopfer @stefbonnet @steffenson @StefMoore
@StefSchumann @stegibson @SteinbrecherInc @Steinhude @steitiyeh @stella_design @Stella_Hernandz @stellaokc @StellarStrategy @StellasBlossoms @stellavision
@stelzner @stemcellshealth @steph_begley @stephaniec2c @stephaniecombs @StephanieDeneke @StephanieDM88 @StephanieFrank @StephanieJHale @StephanieMater
@StephanieMDavis @StephanieNickel @StephaniePeck @stephanieshott @stephanieswann @StephanieWatson @StephanyPuno @StephCalahan @Stephen_ATN
@Stephen_Bray @stephen_dan @StephenBienko @stephenbsanders @StephenClinton @stephencoles @StephenCourt @stephencurtin @stephendaviscxo @stephendebruyn
@stephenkruiser @stephenleesings @stephenlynch @stephenodonnell @StephenRPohlit @stephensmith3 @StephenWelton @StephenWLarson @stephgreenkc
@Stephie_Lewis @stephsammons @StephSouthwick @StepIntoChina @StereoStone @SterlingFive @SterlingMail @SternalPR @StetsonU @steube @steve_dodd @steve_hartkopf
@Steve_MLM_Jones @Steve_SEO_UK @Steve_Wakefield @steve_ward @steve1johnson @SteveAkinsSEO @stevealfaronet @steveant @steveatrma @steveauthentic
@steveb2u @SteveBauer @SteveBreitman @SteveBrossman @stevebuelow @stevecowan @stevedarnell @stevefarber @SteveFrerich @stevegasser @steveglissman
@SteveGrim @SteveGTaylor @SteveHandy @SteveHMills @steveholt27 @SteveInOhio @stevejankowski @SteveKayser @stevekleber @SteveKoss @Stevelemons
@Stevelev17 @SteveLevine1 @SteveLorenzo @SteveMacDonald @SteveManning @SteveMeehan5 @stevemordue @stevemullen @steven_fletcher @Steven_Shaw
@StevenALowe @stevenaquaffect @stevenbrubaker @StevenBrun @StevenDownward @STEVENETWORK @StevenFudd @stevenfung @stevengiles @stevengmiller
@stevengoforth @stevenhealey @StevenHudson @StevenBiz @StevenLSnyder @stevenmills70 @stevenpmeadows @StevenRobello @stevenroddy @StevenRothberg
@stevensanchez3 @StevenSchlagel @stevenseagul @stevenwagstaff @steveohscereal @Steveology @stevepohlit @SteveRosenbaum @SteveRothaus @SteveSaimon
@stevesipress @SteveSmith_Cake @SteveSmorgon @stevesoma @SteveStelzner @stevethegoose @stevetheseeker @SteveTN @stevetuf @steveuk007 @SteveVale
@SteveWoda @stevez33 @stevie11 @steviedove @StevieSays @steview @stewartb2b @StewartwWilson @StewySongs @StGeorgeCreativ @sthBodyJewelry @sticviews
@stiennon @StillettoChick @stillgoingon @stillsafe @StillSoftVoice @stillsoul @stimulusaccess @StinkingRoseLA @stinman @stirlingbond @STISingles @StitcherDeb
@stitchkingdom @StKonrath @STLChildrens @StLmate @StLNetworkGuru @StLouisBloggers @stlsmr @StMaartenDivers @StMarysU @stmnetwork @stoansteirer
@Stoccado @stockaplus @StockGoodies @StockGoodies1 @stockinvestor2 @stockmarketing @stocknetwork @stockphotog @StocksDiva @StockSolution @Stocksox
@StockStrategies @StockTalkRadio @StocktonBOGO @StockTweeters @stocktwiterpick @StockyardsTexas @StokerAllure @StolenDogs @StoneCS @stonedlogic
@StoneleighHotel @stonepimp @stoneteam1 @stoneWoodOutlet @Stonyfield @StopBitingNails @stopsigntweets @stopsnoringtips @StopTheHike @stopthepolitics
@Storage_News @StorageMonkeys @StorageNeighbor @storebrowser @Storenvy @storeprofits @Stormi18 @StoryofMyLife @StoryWorldwide @StowasserFranz
@str8photography @str8tbiotch @stradablog @StraightSimon @strandstoelen @strange_surpris @strat1k @Strategic_Web @StrategicAdvice @strategicsense @strategywebd
@StratLearner @stratovaari @Stratspecialist @strawberry_luv @StreamedMovies @streamingepisod @streamingmarv @StreamiumTweets @streamlabel @StreamlineFS
@streetadsmedia2 @streetforce1 @StreetKingEnt @Streetmachine @StreetReeves @STREETwear_ @stremcha @StressFreeBill @StressFreeCook @stressless @StrikeBowling
@Strikerphil @strongcitytech @stronghuman @StrongmanTweets @stroupsam @StructuredMindz @strulowitz @StuartDMT @stuartfeigley @stuartflatt @stuartlaing
@stuartlockley @StuartMilton @stuarttan @StuartZadel @stubsy315 @Stuck_Together @StudentLifeOC @StudentMindPwr @students4money @studio_automate @studio525
@StudiodiMare @studiomoviegril @Studios92_ @StudyDroid @StudyingAbroad @studyingskills @stuffmagazine @stulrix @StuMcMullin @stuntmenmovie @StureNyberg
@sturg58 @StuSmaab @StuWeinstock @stweetdeals @stweetSHAUNA @STXherry @styledo @styleontherun @styleshark @stylishlyme @stylishtalk @StyriaEventscom
@suarezmoises @sub5mango @subashs @subbujois @subliminalvideo @submit_articles @submitexpress @SubmitWizard @subq @SubsFrisco @Suburban_Farmer
@suburbanmama @suburbansurvive @SuburbanWines @suburbview @SubZeroService @Success__Secret @Success_4_All @success_brenda @Success_Search
@Success_with_BP @successadvisor @successbiz @SuccessBooks @SuccessCoachNJ @SuccessExpo @SuccessFit @successforum @successfulmlm @successify
@Successmate @successnation @successtab @successtrategy @SuccessTutor @successwalls @SuccessWithMike @succuoach @ @sudharsanece @sudiptaroy @sue_oshea
@sueandsteve @SueAwesome @sueballmann @sueblaney @suecartwright @suegresham @sueissilly @suekearney @SueMarks @suendercafe @SueRileyRealty
@SueScaletta @suevanfleet @sueyoungmedia @suffrena @suganINDIA @Sugar_Smash @SugarDee @SugarfootRock @SugarJones @sugeshg @SuggestionBox @sugoiasiangirl
@suhel_khan @SujataChadha @SujataKohli @sumal @sumaya @summer_goodwin @Summer_of_egypt @summersidePEI @summitlifecoach @SummittBusiness
@sun_and_Beach_ @SundanceSuccess @SunDiety @sundognet @Sung_H_Lee @SunilJaiswal @SunitaRaheja @SunLifeGuys @SunMergers @SunnyRainer @SunnyThoughts
@SunRemuServices @SunriseFiction @sunryyse_tw @SunsetMotorsLA @sunshail @Sunshine3108 @sunshinegrounds @sunshineserious @SunStudioLA @sunti_wide
@SunWarrior @SupAcademy @Suparnamalhotra @super_mango @SuperAffiliateC @SuperAffiliateI @SUPERbau @superbowlsmash @SupercoolAgency @superdupershark
@superearners @SuperEB @SuperFairyQueen @SuperFlySteve @SuperGirl @SuperHeroPS @superhomebiz @superiorpayday @superkiing @Superkoala_FR @Superlearning
@SupermanLovesU @supermom_in_ny @supermoms @superonlineman @SuperParentMom @SuperShopperorg @supertdownloads @Superyax @SupJoseph @suplementa
@SupplyChainBlog @SupporterHAITI @SupportShidonii @SupportUSForces @supremeluxe @Supt_surcease @SupWeekly @SurajOpenBook @SurfAds @surfcanyon
@SurfCorp @Surfettes @surffans @surfFit @SurfGirlBrit @surfingchef @surfingmaniac @surfjar @SurfRecession @SurfSportsCoach @surfster99 @surfvoucher @SurgeryUSA
@SurgiSil @surrealchicago @SurRylgroup @survey4u @surveysam @SurveysRock @Surya_Source @susan_boyle_com @Susan_Cox @Susan_Eller @Susan_Hopper
@susan_neonlily @Susan_Nicol @Susan_OHara @susan300tweets @SusanBonfiglio @SusanBoylesCat @SusanCareerTrek @SusanCosmos @SusanCritelli @susandore
@susanemeadmh @SusanFinco @susangilmore @susangiurleo @susanhaimet @susanhanshaw @susanjarema @SusanKovalesky @SusanMazza @susannegriffing
@susannewcomer @SusanOdev @SusanPreston @susanroane @SusanSargood @susansoaps @susantellem @susanwilson39 @susaye @susbizleaders @susby @Sushi_Zushi
@sushilpunia @sushisurfer @susianelucena @susiecheng @susiequilter @susiescarth @susihendarti @sustainableweb @SustainSites @susybb @Sutclip1957 @SuuperG
@SuzanaPR @Suzanne_Lavigne @SuzanneH110 @suzannekattau @suzannepeters @SuzanneShaffer @suzanschmitt @suzi_fairbairn @SuzieCheel @suzieholmes @SuziMorris
@suziphillips @suzipomerantz @suzmccormick @SuzooMukherjee @suzukiofwichita @suzyspaatz @suzyturn @svartling @svb @svcprodirect @SvenJohnston @svennyg
@svenschweizer @svera1ny @svitasek @Swag_Web_Design @SwagTips101 @swallow_town @SwamiCity @SwamiScotty @SwampSchool @swampy52 @SwanBlog
@SwankyPaper @swapalease @swarnavarb @swarnaw @swarrman @swarup @SWAT_Institute @swaygrl @SWBizCom @swbuyers @swedal @Sweden_United
@SwedishGirlLisa @swee06840 @sweet_chris23 @sweet_mallows @sweetdebbie101 @sweeters14 @SweetEsKitchen @sweethoneybee6 @SweetLeafTV
@SweetMarketing @sweetnsexy210 @SweetRetreatHC @sweetsfoods @SweetSoaps @SweetSue @sweetwatersavin @SweetzMarshall @swentz @Sweta6 @swetha190
@swhitegrass @swierm @SwiftIncome @Swiggs @SwirllWine @swissbusiness @swisschasy @SwissTourism @switchyourhouse @SWITTERmrossi @swjetski_rental @SWJS
@swmcon @swonderlin @swopper_news @SWSF @SWTulsa @SXM_Intern @Sybil_B @SyedmRaza @syifamukdas @Sylvia_Cheong @sylviabrowder @SylviaBuetow
@SylviaPerreault @sylviavillagran @SylvieDahl @sylwilson @Symfonic @SympoOBGYN @synapseone @synaurabusiness @SyncCreation @syndicatescoop
@SYNERGYCLUBS @synergyofmind @SynergySG @Syracusejobs @SysCommUK @SysCorp @syseda @SystemSociety @sytru @Sze_Lee @sztorinethu @t_asia
@T_Harv_Eker @t_retoevents @T_RoyJackson @t0dds @t18u @T2TNetworkCom @T3CHN0L0GIC @t5blog @TaaDaaGina @TAB_ZThree @tabat @Table4Five2
@TablesFurniture @taboohairsalon @TachelleDaniels @Tacklesaver @Taco_Bueno @TacticalContact @tagnest_au @TAGoldMine @TAH99 @tahoeblu @TaigaCompany
@tairby @takatezu @take26media0 @Take2seconds @takeaction2 @takeastand @TakeMeNational @takemoneyfree @TakeThe_Plunge @TakeTheNextStep @takingchargenow
@takisrs @taksu33 @Talenpalet1 @TalentArrow @TalentAsia @TalentCulture @TalentFishInc @TalentHook @TalentTalks @talenttribes @TaliGillette @talk_business
@talk2brazil @TalKamal @TalkDebbie @TalkDisney @Talkin_Sport @TalkShowNews @TalkwithTracy @TallChicknVegas @tallshipp @Talya @tamagawl @TamalanehH
@tamara_cobbin @TamaraFulcher @TamaraW_2 @tamcdonald @tamebay @TamelaJaeger @tamhajerry @TamiAtVCConnex @tamihonesty @TamiSchiller @Tammie_Nielsen
@TammyAndFriends @TammyBurnell @TammyLandau @tammymoore @TammySievers @tammyuy @tammywjones @tampico @Tampogonow @tamrataylor @tamuken
@Tanamaree @tanay46 @TAndersonAZ @Tangara @tangerinesalons @taniawil @tankbiz @tankforyou @TannersDad @TantricMaster @tanyamarie13 @TanyaSahota
@taohero @tapaslunchco @tappetalk @tapsearcher @Tara__S @tara_camp @Tara_Nelson @taracarbo @TARAdactyl @TarahFO @TaraHolling @TaraKachaturoff
@TaraLangey @Taramichener @tarantellamedia @tarapos @tarasgetz @tarasview @taraturk1 @tarekmohamed @targetedprofits @TargetLatino @TargetStars @TARHhhhh
@tarrell69 @tarrikjackson @tarshajacksonva @TART_Bakery @tarungupta1989 @TarynP @TarzanRusso @TaserPartyGirl @Tashaeva @TashaIghodaro @tashamma @tashcast
@TashiGonpo108 @Tasi_Lima @TaskRabbit @TaskStreetTeam @TasteAddison @tasteforcooking @TasteForLife @tasteNZ @tasteofaz @tastetvnetwork @TatianaGonzalez
@tatopu @TattooLifestyle @TattooRebel @Tattoos2 @TauhidahL @TauhidChappell @tauhidul @Taurus3DLogos @tavanloc @tavomi15 @tax_me_less @taxgirl
@taxhelprightnow @taxhelpukcom @TaxPro2HelpYou @taxresolution @taxreturnuk @taxtherapy @Taxthink @taxtweeter @TaydeAburto @tayfilms @Taylor_Robins
@tayloredassess @taylorfyhrie @Taylorjordinn @taylormadeideas @TaylorMntr @TaylorRMarshall @TayoRockson @tayuda @TazSolutions @tbctainment @TBilich
@TBMMinc @tbouchey @tboyum @tbranchsolution @TC_Lowe @TC247_Networks @tcaoitTW @Tcat @tchinformer @TCLMarshals @TCMortgage @tcmtweet @TCo070
@TCo077 @TCo777 @tcotchat @TCS_biz @TCSKINNER @tcstamara @TCTaxTeaParty @TCusack247 @TD_TestBot @tdanford @tdcinhawaii @tdgobux @tdisanza
@TdotHuskies @tdowns1964 @tdwusavalues @TeaBreakCrumbs @teachalotgirl @Teachersgrammar @teachinghands @TeachMeGP @teachmejordan @teachmetech
@Teachtofreedom @TeacupGardener @Teafft @Tealow @Team_Grandma @TeamAverageJoe @TeamBeadlesIndo @teambuild @TeamBuildingPro @teamDaphnes @teamfactor
@TeamKay @teamkreate @TeamMarketing @TeamMerkaba @Teamplayer02 @teamplayer14 @teampyxism @TeamSurgical @teamtobinhomes @TeamWBC @TeamworkRadio
@TeamworkTimG @Teapartier2010 @teapartysigns @teapriestess @TEApublican @teastal @tecdat3 @Tech_Bit @TechArmy @TechChunks @techclubcpr @TechCoach
@TechEEZ @TechFrog @techglance @techintwenty @TechLemmings @techmashup @techmedicus2 @technewsmiw @TechnicaGroep @TechniCOWL @Technisource
@technocrom @TechnoEvanGuy @technomania @TechnoPaganism @technopodge @TechnoScotty @Techonomics1 @techpinas @TechPRMaven @techrecruiterva @techroid
@techsavvychic @TechShali @TechToolGuru @techtools4re @techydude46 @TechyTommy @TechZader @TechZoomIn @TECMidwest @ted_mcgrath @tedbradford2
@tedcoine @TeddyTester @TeddyTowncrier @TedInJest @tedkinzer @tedmurphy @TedNguyen @TedRobertson @TedRubin @tedsv @TEDxB @TEENchirp @TeenDomainer
@teendotvn @teenfabulous @Tegart @tegernsee_tv @tehnoskomputi @tehostamo @TeitoKlein @tejas74 @tejones @TEK2_CARDS @tekany @TekBz @TEKGROUP
@tekkieblog @teknews @telamony @Tele_Watch @TeleCollege @TelecomRush @TelecomSpe @telekton @teletrack @teliaco @TellaFriend @Tellem @tellmethursday
@teltub_daily @temacafe1000 @temazo @TembuaLanguage @TemerityMag @temhideki @TemperedMC @TemplateCascade @templehayes @tenaciousartist @tencredit
@tenfacesofshe @tengreenones @TenPercentLegal @tentop10 @TenutaVitanza @TeoGelato @TeppoT @TequilaRack @TeraRecipes @tercerowines @terencechung
@terencedwards @Teresa_MrsB @teresaberry @TeresaCleveland @teresacuervo @TeresaFBarrett @TeresasFengShui @TeresaSimons @teresawhite @teri_sawers @teridusold
@TeriGatarz @terilg @terimorris @teripayne @TerjeSkakstad @term_papers @terner6 @Terraellen @Terrance247 @TerranceCharles @TerranceDJones @terrasantapr
@TerraSD @TerrellSandefur @TerrenceYoung @terriclay @TerriDolan @TerriKosecki @Terrillific @terrimcculloch @terripark @Terry_Allison @terry_levine @Terry_Long @
TerryAlmond @terrycoker @terryjbrown @TerryJett @TerryLawFirm @terryloving @terrymarkle @terrymslobodian @terrypetrovick @terryptb @terrystarkey1 @TerryTheJet
@TerryUnrau @TerryVoth @TerryWygal @terunghijau @TeruoArtistry @Tessazan @TesslerPT @teteroces @tetka @Tetsuya_K @tevaloa @tevami @texanrose @Texaplex
@Texas_News @Texas4god @TexasBarBooks @texasdefensive @TexasGarabedian @TexasGrand @texashealth_jen @Texasholly @TexasJackFlash @TexasLegendsNBA
@TexasLending @texasmag @TexasPhotoBooth @texasranchscape @TexasRV @TexasTavern @TexasTech @TexasTripper @TexasWineTweets @texeyes @Texfoot
@Text4Cocktails @textlicious @textopportunity @textprovider @texttogift @TezOsman @tfdu @TferThomas @tfhall @TFInternational @TGarzaPhotog @tginnett @tgmason
@th_watches @ThaiisR @ThaiVest @ThalesPrado @ThaLoveOfMoney @Thames21 @thamusicmaster @thankuthursday @ThanMerrill @TharaldsonHosp @ThaRealMisfit
@That_DanRyan @ThatDamnKwash @ThatFeelsNICE2 @thatMLMbeat @ThatPRGirl @thatreallybites @thatsbusiness @thatspeaker @thattalldude @thatwoman_is

@ThaVM @ThBusinessCoach @thdon @THE__MVP @The_Amplifetes @the_antitweet @The_CLA_Group @The_Dallas_Man @the_dubsters @the_jamielynn @The_Jerri_Ann @the_kid1130 @the_killer65 @The_Life_Coach @the_nose @The_Proposal @the_RT_guy @The_Seeder @The_Social_CEO @The_Thunderbolt @the_vinci @the_wallpapers @the33news @the3rdgoal @TheAaronBowley @TheAbramson @theabundantgift @TheaClay @TheActingCenter @TheAdolphus @theahaguy @theairportvalet @theajayieffect @thealphafemme @theantijared @theAOMC @TheArrivalGuide @theartoflaw @TheAssistant4u @theaterprogram @TheatreIV @thebabyelmoshow @thebachelorguy @thebandwagonfw @TheBasookaBoys @TheBBWPersonals @thebeachshow @TheBeanCast @thebeaverhousen @thebetterlife @TheBibleGuy @TheBigfella @TheBigKlosowski @thebikenut @thebitbit @THEBLASTINGCAP @TheBodTEAShop @thebodyknows @TheBoffinTeam @theboxlounge @TheBreastCancer @TheBritishTexan @TheBuddhaWay @TheBumpMeister @thebutterlife @TheBuzzinator @Thecamecenter @thecandlelady @TheCardWoman @TheCatCo @thechannelc @thechimachine @TheChrisDockery @thecircuit_ @theclickbankcde @TheClineGroup @TheCoffeeKlatch @TheComedyShop @TheCommonGolfer @TheCommonHoster @TheCompEdge @TheCompWizard @TheConceptWhiz @TheConcupiscent @TheCoolestCool @thecopypro @TheCosmonaut @TheCrazyOleMan @TheCrexent @TheCRMGuy @thecrowies @TheCupcakeBlog @thecurelist @TheCVClinic @thecwordagency @TheDailyBlonde @TheDailyWoman @TheDanaReport @TheDapAffect @TheDaringWoman @TheDateSafeTeam @TheDawsonMethod @TheDesertrose @thediaperbaker @TheDietAdvisors @TheDigitalDoctr @TheDigiWAVE @TheDiviGroup @thedogmeister @thedomesticdiva @thedoodlemoodle @thedoomsday @TheDoorClubs @TheDougAnderson @thedroidguy @TheDrop @thedropshipper @TheDuffyAgency @TheDukeofEarle @thee2012 @TheECI @TheEgoExpert @theeMailguide @TheEndReview @TheExpert @TheFactRemains @thefatigue @TheFeinsteins @TheFifthDriver @TheFirstCup @TheFirstTeeLR @TheFishCatcher @thefloorbroker @theflyingchange @THEFLYLADY @thefolllower @thefollowking @thefoodcurb @thefoodwarrior @thefootballnut @theForexArticle @thefoundationau @TheFreeGazette @TheFrownies @thefrugalchef @theFullNoise @TheFundingGuru @thefutureisred @TheGadgetHound @TheGadgetStack @TheGaming411 @TheGazzMan @thegiftlady @TheGLDC @thegoddelusion @TheGoldenhearts @TheGoodOnes_srl @TheGoToSite @thegrammardoc @thegrandcinema @TheGreatDanaJ @thegreenchick @TheGreenHome @TheGreenOTCBB @TheGreenPM @thegreenslam @thegregbell @TheGscape @TheGuruGirls @TheGutes @TheGymCoach @thehalloffamers @TheHandymanPro @thehannaclarke @thehappypainter @TheHealthJunky @theheartofArt @TheHenry @thehilltweets @TheHippieDiva @TheHolmesGroup @TheHomeBizWoman @TheHotSociety3 @TheHRExpert_Sam @thehrgoddess @theHRmaven @thehrphenomenal @thehrstore @thehulkster @TheHWFactor @theimpactzone @theIMStrategy @TheInspirista @TheIntelligentW @theintelligiser @TheInterviewPro @TheInterzone @TheJanF @TheJASMblog @TheJayJones @thejeffkaller @TheJeffNeil @TheJeffWagner @thejimjams @TheJimmyHart @thejobmatch @theJogarGroup @thejondaniels @thejoule @TheJoyntChicago @thejuicywoman @TheKansan_News @TheKarleeStar @TheKayWay @thekells @thekevincouch @TheKidsDoctor @thekillertweets @thekindlekraze @thekindlestop @TheKingsGinger @thekjacrew @TheKrabb @thelamestdotcom @thelaptopgeek @thelastshow @TheLauraJackson @TheLazyMan @TheLeaderLab @TheLeadShop @TheLemonadeBoy @TheLesbianMafia @TheLifeofPower @TheLinkedinGuy @TheListGuy @thelivingwork @TheImaBaker @ThelmaDreyer @thelocaltourist @TheLoging @TheLouRecruiter @thelundgrengang @TheLundy @TheLVTweetUP @TheMadeBed @TheMark1000 @TheMartaReport @themartinidiva @TheMarvelman1 @themattymiller @TheMDBrand @themediamatters @themediamogul @themeetmarket @themelib @Themelis_Cuiper @themestyles @TheMetroMom @TheMisfitsRep @TheMissionSpec @TheMitchellz @TheMommaGuide @TheMoneyDealer @TheMontereyCo @themoversreview @themoviepool @theMRC @TheMsAnonymous @TheMuscats @THEMUSTANG @Themwap @TheNameEngine @thenameshopnz @TheNeelGroup @TheNegotiator @TheNetConnector @thenetshop @TheNewsChick @TheNextFollower @thenorthernedge @theoaksatboca @theoddnumbers @TheoHanden @theoilMD @TheOldFarmHouse @TheOmahaBeef @TheOnion_ @theonlinebizman @TheOnlineMLM8 @Theonlygoodguy @TheOperaInsider @theopportunity @TheOregonianBoo @TheORing_360 @TheOysters @TheParentHive @ThePastime @ThePetPip @ThePetPortal @thephillife @thephotoargus @thepianomarket @thepizzaexpert @theplanetd @ThePMCoach @thepokerusablog @ThePondJumper @ThePresentCo @ThePrettyBxtch @thePRguycom @ThePriceGroup @thePrintDaddy @theprintlounge @theprjkt @TheProfit @TheProfitShare @thepropertybiz @THEpropertyDiva @TheProphetBar @ThePRwriter @thequotewhore @TheQwoffBoys @therabreath @TherapyBabeAZ @TherapyDogGabe @TherapyOnline @therealamyzents @TheRealJFella @therealkazia @TheRealMenice @therealmfb @theredrecruiter @theredstapler @TheReelCritics @theresabaiocco @theresadowning @TheresaDurrant @theresajohnson @theresajones @TheresaLargusa @ThereseMiu @theresumechick @TheResumeMama @theresumewriter @TheRichardScott @therichman001 @TheRiseToTheTop @TheRoomMovie @TheRoxor @theroxy @therriensecure @TheRudeTypist @TheRudyReport @TheSantaYnezInn @thesatorigroup @thesavingqueen @TheSavvyDoc @thesavvyseller @theschoolbag @thescoop1 @thescottbishop @TheSeanTucker @thesearchagents @TheSearchGuru @thesecretbrasil @TheSecretLOA @theSeobaba @TheSEOGenie @TheshanAlwis @theshearsfamily @TheShyMuse @thesidestrip @thesilverbarn @TheSiteMap @TheSkinSociety @Thesmallvoice @thesmmguru @TheSocial_1 @thesocialbiddy @TheSocialCHRO @TheSocialCMO @thesocialpro @TheSocialSquad @TheSocMediaPro @thesolarcoach @TheSolardiva @theSongLine @thesoulchick @thespecific @thestinkingrose @TheStockScout @thestocktweets @thestocktwiter @thestreetsiknow @thesuccesszone @Theta_Miracles @TheTASCGroup @theteachingbox @thetearooms @theteeshirts @TheTerzaFactor @TheThirdStage @thetich @thetico411 @thetigerdouble @TheTinyJEWELBox @thetoiletpaper @TheTonyChan @TheTravelEditor @thetravelsecret @thetweet_tank @TheTweet_tanks @thetweetcheckr @thetweetiegirl @thetweettanklen @TheTweetTankone @thetwinkieaward @TheUMS @TheUNPAclub @TheUWC @TheValentyne @TheVCF @theVETRecruiter @thevikings @theVIPERroom @TheWarriorSage @TheWatersAgency @TheWealthyCop @thewebchef @TheWebRockstar @TheWebWarrior @theweddingproje @thewhalehunters @TheWhistlingElk @TheWineWhore @thewiredserf @TheWisdomCrowds @TheWizardofO @TheWomensMuseum @thewritersroad @thewritingcode @thextremebitz @TheYaffeGroup @TheYandR_Lady @theyne @theyoungdread @TheYoungTurks @TheZenBull @TheZuckerTeam @ThierrySmeekes @Things2sell @thingstotweet @thinkbigKC @ThinkBigNow @thinkbsg @ThinkBusiness @ThinkCausality @ThinkCignal @ThinkingCoach @ThinkInNewAreas @thinkproductive @ThinkPyxl @thinkreferrals @thinktosucceed @thinkvaulter @ThinkWithSatish @thinkyourmoney @thirddoor @ThirdSectorLab @thirstyfishinfo @ThirtyOne_Gifts @ThisDayInRock @thisdotthat @thisgoodriddle @thisisjustin @thisismattball @thisistokyo @ThisnThatBlog @THmelar @thomannITZ @Thomas_Weil @Thomas0985 @thomas3762 @thomascarroll @thomascjensen @thomascook @ThomasGordonONE @thomasjames201 @ThomasKastor @ThomasKish @thomasmarzano @ThomasMcEvoy @thomasrieke @thomasrobinson1 @ThomasShea @ThomasShort2334 @ThomasTimely @thomaswigington @ThommiOdom @ThomRainer @ThomScott @thomswartwood @Thotpot @thoughtLEADERS @ThoughtPartner @thoward @thpeppermntleaf @thprwil @Three_Ten @Threedot @ThreeGirlsMedia @threestonefire @ThriftyVault @thrillbuys @thrillophilia @thtlighting @thubten @THull @ThumpNetwork @ThunderandBlood @thuypro @Thwapr @Tia_Mateo @TiaDobi @TIBET_BUDDHISM @TiciaEvans @tickethaters @Ticketmaster @TicketOS @TickleLipoNow @TickStream @TickTocKs @ticopost @TiDoma @TiEcon @tiefmesser @tiegsj @Tiemorch @Tientjesnet @TifaLockhart @tifanny_g @tifastrife17 @TiffaniBear @TiffanieTillman @tiffanycarlen @TiffanyEckhardt @TiffanyHo @TiffanyLacy @tifftaylorx @TigerEye_MLM @TigerFanatics @tigernow @tigerwoodsman @TigerYung @tiggertagger @tiggio @TiheiMauriora @tijuanaHavenhil @tikanew @TikejaOnline @tikilis @tilakhira @tilphotoNorway @Tim_Long @tim_malone @tim_woods @tim8155 @timacummins @timandjulie @timastevens @TimAtkinson_ @timbay @TimBesecker @Timbofoster @TimBonds @TimBransford @timbruner @timcarter @TimClowers @TimDanyo @TimDarnellAC @TimDebronsky @Time2Design @time2evolvit @Time2LivYRvison @timeapplication @timeclockman @TimeforLifeVA @TimeOutMom @timepicks @TimeshareExit @TimeToGetYours @TimeToGoVirtual @timfrick @timheeney @TimJensen @timjonesdenver @TimLovitt @TimMoore @TimmyBx @TimmyRex @TimmySabre @Timocrat @TimoJappinen @timonlinementor @TimothyBlack @TimothyBurke @TimothyCaron @TimothyEnalls @timotis @TimRandle @TimRedmond @TimSackett @timsander @Timsociety @TimsStrategy @TimSteamboat @timsthomas @timtaxde @TimTyus @TimWoda @tina_w_hudson @TinaBradfordPR @TinaCook @TinaGonda @tinakouts @TinaLouise16 @TinaMc @tinamills @tinammichaud @TinaPFoster @tinastullracing @TinHangLiu @Tinu @TinyDancer500 @Tips4BecomeRich @tipshowtomake @TIQ1 @Tirgumit @tiroaconsulting @Tis_Himslf @tishyb @TitaSGarcia @Tiwankiw @TiXiTBox @TizJustCool @TizJustStupid @TJBillings @tjbuffoonery @TJCarter02 @TJeffersonQuote @tjholthaus @tjhuckabee @TJMcCue @tjnowak1 @TJNTIY @tjones0 @tjowens1 @tjsitback @tjstaab @tjuan @TKarlMiller @tkellenaers @TKFwriter @tkinder @tkireilis @tkmoss @tkolsto @tkpleslie @tkripas @tkung @TLBaker1 @TLCxHOME @tlindorfer @TLOTL @tlpeery @TLS_Marketing @TLWH @tmaduri @tmantra @tmariebrown @TMarieHilton @TMatlack @tmattis67 @tmblairla @tmcbeliever @tmchappy @tmclain @tmcprdctns @tmctyping @TMGmedia @TMHComputer @tmjhelp @tmmJill @tmmywllms @tmonhollon @tmopperman @tmoreira @tmpfeiffer @tmpollard @tmraider @TMRDirect @TMS_Apps @tmsilvers @tnash77 @tnbasant @TNbase @tnchocolatier @tnmg4u @tnooz @TNR01 @Tobaccokills @tobefreeman @tobey4 @TobiKingsley @tobyparkins @ToccaraLuv @tod_bods @Today_Coupon @todayisdifferen @todaysgiveaways @todaysgolfdeal @todd_herman @Todd_Rutledge @toddafoster @toddbesser @ToddBrink @ToddGellman @ToddGilmore @toddhuff123 @ToddMGreene @toddmintz @ToddMuffley @ToddPLamb @ToddPosey @toddschlomer @toddschnick @ToddTilley @toddvo @ToddZebert @ToDoInDallas @ToDoInDFW @Toewie @togetherdating @togetherwf @Togzee @tojuchem @Tolis_Potiomkin @Toltecjohn @Tom_Brumpton_PR @Tom_Duke @Tom_John @tom_mcleod @Tom_Messett @tom_siwik @Tom_Strebbot @Tom_Zegan_ @ToMakeMoneyInfo @TomAllen1965 @tomallinder @TomAntion @tomaslau @tombed @tomblanco @tombolt @TomBrooks1211 @TomBuford @tomcanning @tomchand @TOMCOGroup @TomConvers @TomDickson @TomDoherty @TomDuong @TomEHenderson @TomEllisAB @tomesimpson @tomfeyer @TomFlowerPro @tomhaney @TomHangs @TomHaupt @TomHCAnderson @TomHumbarger @tominsky @tomkeating @tomleblanc0124 @TomMalesic @TomMangone @TomMartin @tommclash @tommur @tommycummings @TommyKovatch @tommylinsley @tommythomas1523 @tommytrc @TommyWierper @tommyworld @tomotake1873 @Tomplay @tomremington @tomretterbusch @TomRoyce @TomSalataLaw @tomschaepper @tomsebastiani @TomsRiverHomes @TomStrignano @TomSwift @tomthielman @tomtravel2 @TomTuohy @tomturnbull @tomupton33 @tomveo @tomweir_usa2day @ToNcHy_CeCa @tonerdiva @TonerForAutism @toneyfitzgerald @ToniBahn @tonibirdsong @tonicascio @ToniHoffmann @tonipalone @ToniShrader @TonkaPR @Tonny3 @tonton_mtl @Tony_Dao @Tony_van_Kessel @Tony_Verde @tonyadam57 @TonyAlverio @TonyAtDQ @tonybeach @TonyBurroughs @tonyburrus @TonyChacheres @tonydbaker @TonyDiCostanzo @tonydisanza @tonyeldridge @tonygates44 @tonylogue @tonylongo @TonyMackGD @TonyMarino @tonymorganlive @TonymZito @tonynwright @tonypchicago @tonypisano @tonyrgee @TonyRobbinsFans @tonysfi @tonyshan @tonystevens4 @TonyStorti @tonyuk42 @TonyValkov @TonyZito5_37 @tools_seo @toon_c @toonga @TooNiceStocks @toonkerssemaker @Toonmix @toothfairycall @top_body @Top_Lanches @Top100PSStores @top20reos @top500listpromo @TopAchievers @topbananas @TopBibleVerses @TopCameraReview @topcashcow @TopCashGifting @topcasinos4u @topchoise @TopDogNews @TopDollar1000 @TopEmailMarket @topfloorstudio @topgrowthstock @TopGunMLM @TopHitPerfume @TopLinked @TopMarketingTip @topmastermind @TOPpercent @TopProperties @toprecruiters @topsalesmaker @TopSec1 @topsecrets4u @topseoservices @TopStarDiamond @TopTravelAsia @TopTVITeam @TopTweeterTools @TopUserRetweets @Torch762 @torchingigloos @ToriJarvis @ToriJohnson @tornadotorino @tornow @Toronto_PR_Guy @TorontoCityNews @TorontoTruth @TorPix @TorreSex @torsten_panzer @TorstenNeumann @torvijs @toryradio @ToshikaR @ToshioShoko @toshreekant @toskana @tostina @tosyali @Total_Rewards @Totalinvest @totallychadders @TotalRealEstate @totaltennis @TotalViperNet @totc @ToThink @totruck @TouchingWood @touchkarma @touchscreenfad @touchygirl @Tourismstudents @TouristCroatia @touristtracker @TourLafayetteLA @Tournantinc @tours4fun @tourscotland @towelfolding @Towens149 @TownMeDallas @tox125 @toxic_stores @Toy_Joy @toyinosunlaja @ToyotaLew @ToysbUs @ToysRUs @tpandika @TPEntrepreneur @tpettis @tpholmes @TPinkCouture @TPO_Hisself @TPOs_BlogList @TPOs_Favorites @TPPCtv @tpr2 @tr1sh @traackr @Trace_Cohen @TraceTV @TraceyBruns @TraceyCJones @TraceyDelCamp @TraceyMMOwen @traceynile @TraciAspe @tracie914 @traciehoward44 @TraciGregory @traciking @tracitoguchi @trackur @tracmaroney @tracy_tp @Tracy_White_ @tracyandmatt @TracyBN @TracyBrinkmann @tracyclancy @tracydecicco @tracydiziere @TracyGazzard @TracyLiebmann @TracySayWhat @TracyWashington @traddr @TradepalAustin @TradepalBoston @TradepalCLT @TradepalDallas @TradepalIndy @TradepalPhoenix @TradePlumbing @tradercat1 @Traderjoe @TradersLog @TradeShowIdea @TradesLive @tradespot_forex @tradingrichmom @TradUR @traffexone @Traffic_Binge @Traffic_Machine @traffic_queen @traffic2u4free @TrafficGenius @Trafficman60 @TrafficMastery @trafficmills1 @Trafficologist @trafficology @TrafficOnDemand @trafficoweb @traffictoolbelt @TrafficVault @TrafficWaveMail @trailrunnerz @Train4Employers @traindom @TrainerZack @TrainingCKaren @TrainingLoopy @trainingspuls @TrainWithMark @transContext @transparenceweb @TransWorkflow @trappersherwood @travel_life @travel_lover @travel_notebook @traveladvicegal @travelblggr @travelbully @TravelChatForum @traveldeals_usa @TravelDealsNet @traveldudes @TravelFollowers @TravelGator @TravelGoddess4u @travelgrdnsbuzz @TravelGuide_TV @Travelin_Papers @Travelingsingle @TravelingwSusan @Travelinsingle @travelisay @TravelLaneCo @travelmedia @travelnmood @travelonly_Greg @TravelOnPennies

@TravelorShops @travelpodcast @travelrn @TravelsInfo @travelsite1 @traveltipsguy @traveltomaui @TravelToursNow @Traveltron3000 @TravelV @travelwithdayo
@travelwithlisa @travelworldnow @travid @TravisASwain @travisfitzwater @TravisGreenlee @TravisHeinrich @TravisMoffitt @travisro @TravisSharp @TravisWallerCRS
@TRAVSocialMedia @Traz38 @TrazgodKing @TRDimage @TRDonnelly @treasurecoach1 @Treat_ADHD @TrebbauKoop @trebonasomreb @TreceDallas @treedup
@treegiving @treehousei @TRENDadvisor @TrendingCasts @trendsinfo @trendsmagparis @TrendTracker @TrendTweeter @TrendyDC @trentab @trentcox @tresahardt
@TresCoach @TresRiosResort @tressalynne @TrevArmstrong @TreverMcGhee @TrevizoHarrin @TrevNetMedia @TrevorCoxen @trevordierdorff @TrevorSwampy
@trevoryoung @treydalton @treypennington @trgtricities @trialbyjury @TriBabbitt @tribeofnoise @TribeTuesday @Triboda @tribuffalo @Triciachat @trickscorner
@TricksnTips @trickytriskuts @Tricolor_FC @triercompany @TrieuNguyen @trifamenz @TrigamServices @Trigger_Local @TrillionStars @TrilogyPayment @TrimBellyOver40
@triMirror @Trina_Willard @TrinaClaiborne @TrinaKaMarie @TrinaWardell @TrinaWell @TRINI_ZUELEAN @Trinityhall @TrinityIns @trinityriver @trinsicnews
@TriOdysseyGPS @TRIOmedia @TripDawg @TripDucky @triplemast @triplib @tripology @trish_forex @TrishaGary @TrishBeach @TrishDonmall @trishlawrence
@TrishsVoice @trishwalsh66 @triskinity @TriStaff @Tristan_Latge @tristanginnett @TristanrlC @TristaRodeo @TristateVW @TriTecLes @TRIUMPHLVHILTON
@TriumphTitle @TrivaniOnline @Triviable @TrivWorks @TRMeson @TRNUSA @trompyx @TropicalDelight @tropicalgourmet @TropicalMBA @tropicalstormEA
@tropigal @troxellsr @troyajohnson @TroyErickson @troyjensen @troylanderson @troynice @TroyPattee @TroyScheerTMG @trpixman @trpurcell @trsjobs @Truckdrivernews
@TruckerDesiree @truckersteve @truckersutopia @TruckingSpace @truckingsuccess @TrudyKutylo @true_Simona @truebluepatriot @TrueLifeOfBrian @TrueLoveAfter40
@truenaturetrust @truenegative @TrueNorthCustom @TrueShare @trueUvoice @trugem1 @trumpglobal @TrumpMLMNetwork @trumpnetwrkbill @Trumpthat
@Trumpupline1st @truquality @TrustBranding @TrustedCoaching @trustedreferral @truth4girls @truthabs @TruthBellyFat @TruthMission @truthplane @TRW_CreditGroup
@tryantiaging @Trybarefoot @TryBPO @tryin2getfollow @tryingthebiz @tryoneofakind @TrystIndonesia @TSC_Tweets @TSCB @tscochrane @tseamon @TSHaero @tsieck
@tsieger @TSINonprofit @TSONetwork @TsQuest @TStanowski @TsunamiMNetwork @TSXstockpicks @tszymanski @tt904 @ttalola @TTaunya @TTNTeam @ttrenz
@TTwynstra @TubacGolfResort @tubefilter @tubevideo @TubeYouVideo @tubgoddess @TuesdayTip @Tuffour @Tuffylynn @TugaK @TulaHotYoga @TulioRatto
@tunes2901 @TuneTalks @tungvnpt @Tunis @tunisieweb @TupperwareLady @turbo140 @turbobux @turbomarketing @turbomoneygener @TurboSMM @TurboTextAds
@Turfetc @TurkishCoffeeUS @turkmadden @turnagingback @TurnKeyCoach @turnqCEO @TurnSocial @TurtleBayResort @tuscanblog @tushar @tutelage @TutorTina
@tutucasoftware @TuvelComms @TVAspen @tvincome @tvpnr @TVSerials @TW_Design @Tw1tterDynamics @tw1tterschool @twae @Twaitter @twalaxy @twalkin
@twalkr @TwavelTweeter @twaveltwita @twdpm @tweaknotes @Tweal_Estate @Tweash @tweasier @tweecashme @Tweecha_com @tweegoo @tweeneedajob
@tweeple_adder @tweepmarketing @tweepmktg @tweepstats @Tweet_Center @tweet_flirt @tweet_my_biz @tweet_n_win @tweet_programs @Tweet4thecause
@tweetadderdeal @tweetakademie @Tweetalize @TweetAnnounce @tweetaprize @TweetasticBro @TweetAuto @TweetAutomator @tweetbird2 @TweetBizConsult
@tweetboobdude @tweetcaroline @tweetcashing @tweetcashtools @tweetclean @TweetCoachNow @TweetComet @tweetcotton @tweetdal @TweetDeck @tweetdistrict
@tweetdynamite @TweetEchos @tweetemplates @Tweeter2Help @tweeterdiva @tweetermeetings @tweetersforum @TweeterSteele @TweetExploders @tweetfestme
@tweetformoolah @TweetHealthTips @Tweetin4Dummies @tweetinbabe @tweetindollars @Tweeting_Angel @TweetingCHURCH @tweetingdeals @TweetingTools
@tweetinspiratif @TweetItRight @tweetjosht @tweetjunky @tweetlaunch @tweetmaker @TweetmanGary @Tweetmatix @Tweetmoneymoney @tweetmony @tweetmyjobs
@TweetNoke @tweetomatic_de @TweetOnTheRun @TWEEToption @TweetOrTrick @tweetpaste @tweetpiggy @tweetproblems @TweetrafficEZ @tweetrandomizer
@tweetreasures @TweetRiches @tweetrqueen @Tweets2Cash @tweets4living @tweetsandtwits @tweetsarmy @tweetsbot1 @TweetsByUs @tweetsdollars @TWEETSDRAMA
@tweetsformoney3 @TweetsGoneMadUS @tweetsguru @tweetsmagic @TweetSmarter @tweetSponso @TweetStephanie @tweetsteve4cash @tweetsurge @TweetTankGold
@tweettanking @TweetTankMktg @tweettankpro @TweetTex @tweetthisjob @TweetToKnow @Tweettwins @tweetuniversal @tweetupdirectry @tweetusoon @tweetusright
@TweetVerve @tweetVIPmedia @tweetwarpspeed @TweetWeapon @tweetwithbob @Tweetz_traffic @twet101man @twetouch @twettank2gether @Twexperimental
@Twexponential @Tweye @twfaster @twhitaker1974 @TWhiteCreations @twi5 @TwickerSticker @twideoguide @Twience @Twifoo @twig1gy @twiiterguide @Twikimter
@Twilight_Tweetz @TwilightContest @TwilightDesk @twilightersnet @twillydy @twilmott @twimarketing @Twincitysam @TwinGoats @TwinklesJewels @Twinnovate
@TwinPeaksTravel @twistedlime @Twit_Expert @Twit_Jam @Twit2000Barrier @twitaddicted @twitatonui @twitB4U @twitbefriend @TwitBizDay @TwitCashExpert
@TwitchingPuppie @twitdir2000 @twiteconomy @TwiterHero @twiteristic @twiterpro4me @twitersecret @twitfanta @twitfools @twitgoldmine003 @twithawk @Twithear1
@twithope @twitingly @TwitJobsLondon @TwitjobsUK @TwitJumpGuest @twitlinker @TwitMlmTools @TwitMuscle @Twitr_Addict @twitreferral @TwitRestaurants
@twitrfuel @TwitRGolfers @twitRocket @twitrpros @Twitsphere @twitt_erfolg_de @twitt_erlytix @Twitt_inator @twittablestuff @TwittaBling @twittank @twittcash
@TwittConv @Twittegy @TwitterFollower @twittforprofit @twittin4job @twitting_lawyer @TwittInsider @TwittInsights @twittinvestor @twittloans @twittme_mobi
@Twittoing @twittprofit @twittsifu @twitttolllower @twitty7x @twittycash @twiturmarketing @twitwebtester @Twix_Fits @Twixcel01 @twizzersays @TWJCOHA
@twletsmakemoney @twme1 @twocupsconnect @twodigitworld @twollow @twoofusorg @TwooTools @TWOwomenANDaHOE @twpq @TWR_Insights @TwtGuy
@TWTRCON @twtrmoney1 @TwtrPro @TwtrReviews @TwtSecrets @twtultimatebody @Twunique @twuttevaer @twyingout @tx_vacation @TXBirder @txconflictcoach
@txdistancerider @txdivadoll @TXEric @txGarage @TXGrandpa @TxJogger12 @TXLoneStarStaff @txmama @TXMortgages @txmusicchannel @TxRealtor1 @txroadshow
@TXStopsTheSting @txtamsg @TxTough @TxtSpecs @Txtworks @TyBennett @tydomain @TyDowning @tyhychi @tyippie @tyler6914 @tylerbel @TylerDurbin
@TylerFyke @tylrsmllr @typeamom @typelabs @typingbug @TyroneAmerine @tyrstag @tzabaoth @U_Laugh @U_M_A_H @U_together_moon @u2cjb @u4wealth
@UAMSlibrary @uber_apparatus @ubercool @ubergio @Uberoom @UBF_ @ubiquitousrat @UBuyUSA @uc2i @ucminfo @UCYIMD1 @udaypalsingh @UdcBadiaPol
@UEvents @ufginfo @ufgmandura @UGDT @uggbootshop @uggsonline @ugotmojo @ugraesser @ugurarcan @UHartfordNews @uhavebeenserved @uiandme @UIdahoNews
@UISCareerCenter @uk_landlord @UK_Medical_Jobs @UK_SEO @Ukenings @UKJobTweets @uklandforsale @UKPostbox @UKprecision @ukpremier @ulcma
@UlrikeGerloff @ultimateAleks @ultimategadgets @ultoday @ultranex @ultras03 @umairkundi @umarnasir @Umattan @UmbertoTassoni @umbz @uMCLE
@Un_reality @UnaMamaConHijas @unbounce @UncleBobCW @UncleBobsTitle @UncleRick @UncleVicDeals @uncomman @undauctions @Undercover @UndergradReview
@undergroundmk @UndertheDave @UnderTheSunShop @undinecoaching @UndiscoveredStx @undo0720 @UNDRGROUNDHERO @ @unfairconcealin @unfollowtuesday
@unhatched @UniBulMrcntSvcs @unified360 @Unikatemarkt @unilyzer @UniqueArticles @UniqueSynergy @UniqueVitamins @Unisfair @Unisys_Careers @unitedcb
@UnitedTraining @unitedwaydaneco @UnitedWayNola @unitweeter @UniversalAcct @UniversityVisit @unkleEL @unlimited1044 @UnlimitedUsage @UNLOCKmagazine
@UNLVtickets @unreal_g @UnrealCafe @unseenrajasthan @Unsinkable3 @unstickingcoach @unwindbeverage @UofCincyAlumni @UofHartford @UOWHO @uphoria
@upicks @upiqcom @UpMo @uponabranch @uponrequest_oc @UPS_FAIL @UpsideUp @upstartbootcamp @Upstatemomof3 @upthevortex @UptownLaserSkin
@urban_mode @Urban_Springs @urbanapartments @UrbanDecorSue @UrbanElementIN @urbanprojectz @urbansmiler @urbanverve @urbiztopranked @UrFamilyLivin
@URFLIPNOUT @URHealthy2 @urizeldman @urjobcouldbnext @Urlar @URManEnough1 @ursanju @UrthBags @UrviMehta @urwealthwizard @usa_wealth
@usACTIONnews @USAirlinePilots @usamaverick @USANAwealth @USAShopper @USATweetMeets @usbargains @uscapa @USchirodirect @uschles @USCRUDEOIL
@usdmnet @usedequipments @usefultools @UsefulWebApps @useglobalreach @USfestival @USHAREIMG @UshaSliva @Usidus @usmale55 @usmanzk @USNAVYSEALS
@USNMcKinney @USPassenger @ustaymotivated @UStrafficschool @USvisaEasy @utah_analytics @utahaccounting @utahREpro @utahwsoccer @UTAJETS @utamavirod
@utcampusdeals @UTCoverage @UTDBananaKiller @UTDiTella @utegoebels @UteWKing @uthomas68 @utoh @UtopiaComm @Utopical @Utrecht_Art @utterhip
@uuimages @Uurte @Uvindu77 @uVizz @uwelang @uxmag @v_shakthi @V1OLETTE @VA_IT_Jobs @va_mommy @VA_Office @va4hire @vabisin @vacation4
@VacationInfo @vacationkids @vacationnetwork @vacationtribe @VacenTaylor @VAConnections @VacTimesShareRen @vadesktop @VADuff @VAerin @Vagabondangler
@vagabondvistas @VAGirlFriday @Vaiebhav @VAinParadise @ValBloomberg @valentineblog @valentinesstore @valeomarketing @valericcione @Valerie2u @ValerieFM80
@valeriemerrill @valerienichols @ValerieSimon @valiantmedia @valkhot @valleriastracha @ValleryGraham @valmg @ValOlsonCareers @ValPopescu @ValuePagesGroup
@valuesdrivenpro @valukan2 @ValveInteract @VAmatchmaker @Vambry @vampirezoey @vamsri @VanajaGhose @VandaLynnHughes @vandenboomen @vandexter
@VandiverGroup @Vanessa_Green @vanessasanger @vanetworking @vangole @Vanguard_M_G_T @vanialex @vanillacokehead @VanillaIceKid @vannjeffreys @VantageBiz
@VantageLtd @Vanygirl @VaproTweets @varchassri @VArenovations @varinder_seo @various5 @varjuluceno @VarsityBuys @varsitytutors @vascosoares1 @VASERPro
@vashtihorvat @Vasilis02 @Vasilius @vasimpleservice @VAsolutionsNOW @Vassist @VastgoedDirect @VastIIncome @VaszaryGabor @vavangue @vayvi @vb2ae
@vbsondemand @Vcanro @VCI_helps @vcordo @vcubeusa @vddingman @VDmitruk @vdub01 @vedo @veeh1 @veg311 @VegaLawyer @Veganmainstream @VegasBill
@vegasblender @VegasCLEARguy @VegasHouseSale @Vegaspromo @VegasStilettos @vegasventures @VegetarianInfo @VeggieGrill @vegtv @vejalagos @VeJason
@VeloraStudios @VELTINSarena @velvetskirt @vemmakids @VemmaNewhouse @vemmasa_verve @Vendegvaro @VendorSourcing @VenueGen @venusvision
@verdandisquidoo @Vered @Veredusatl @VeretaLee @VergeConsulting @verhaal140 @Veribatim @Veritas_Design @verkauffoerdern @verkoren @VerndaleTweets
@VernonDavis @vernongirl @VernonMack @veronica_duran @VeronicaHay @VeronicaTanBK @VeronikMartinz @Veroniqque @Versatron @Versicherungsde @versustv
@Vertizy @VerveCards @VerveHealthyNRG @Very1967 @VeryCherryCoCo @vest31 @vestival @VeteranWarrior @vetsurvivor @vexyjenna @VGalFriday @vgardening
@VHenry @VHTrabosh @Vhutchisoncoach @viable4u @viaddress @Viadeo @Viakeywest @viamelissa @vianovagroup @VibrantSpirit @vibsters @vic_cholet @vicbarrera
@vicentesaraiva @vices @viciousvst @vicki_s_young @vickicaruana @Vickie_Sayce @Vickie_Smith @vickietolbert @vickijjasper @vickis36 @vickiscannon @VickiSouthard
@VickiZerbee @VickyHennegan @VickyLaney @vickylyn @viclibos @vicmangino @vicnuge @VicoRockMedia @victor_chan @victor_cheng @Victor_Go_Ham
@VictorAntonio @victoreegadgets @victoreme @VictorGanan @victoria_stone1 @victorianetc @victoriarealtor @victoriashortt @victorliew @VictorOcampo @victorpagan
@victorvigil @Victory_Credit @VictoryTavern @vidcom @Video20Q @VideoArmy @videocop @VideoGuruToon @videohustling @VideoMafia @videoministry
@videonacho @videophonervp @videosdoyoutube @videosocialcode @videoturf @vidmagmedia @vidmarketing1 @vidpr @VidPromotion @vidyasdesai @viensa @vieodesign
@vietnamesegirls @vietnammobi @ViewspotNetwork @ViewTV @viikassood @VijayThangaraja @vikasjee @vikaskumar @vikassen @vikingkat @ViktoriaFoxx @Vilallonga
@villageous @VillageShopping @VillainOrHero @VillaO_Dallas @VillTweet @vimel @VinayPaturu @Vince_Craine @VinceAllen @vincebaker @VinceBerthelot @vincedeon
@VinceMayfield @Vincent_Ang @VincentAdams @VincentColes @VincentL @VincentMuir @VincentParker @vincentsmit @vincentvandam @vincentvhelle @vincentwhite
@VincentWright @vineetsblog @viniciusbidarte @VinnieVasquez @Vinothek @vinsalm @VinSolutions @VintageBelt @VintageBelts @ViolaEllsworth @VioletCaren
@Vioroso @VIPazzi @VipeCanada @VIPlifestyle @viprealtydfw @vipregan @vipromoters @vipselling @vipspams @VipSports @viptalent @vipvirtualsols @VIPwealthclub
@viralclix @viraler_effekt @viralfirefly @viralhive @viralmarketing9 @viralmarketmom @viralspirals @viraltube @VirendraSEO @virginiagaga @virginiog @virtnews
@virtualblessing @virtualewit @virtuallinda @VirtuallyAmaz @virtuallyideal1 @virtuallyready @VirtualMarketer @VirtualOfficeB @virtualpartner @virtualpm @VirtualSocial
@virtualtotte @virtuouswoman25 @vishalgarora @vishalgondal @visiatotravel @Vision4Standard @VisionarySpirit @VisionTech_2015 @visionwebnet @visit_dallas
@VisitGalena @VisitGalenaOrg @VisitGBI @visitmytown @visitpuretravel @visomusic @VistageKC @VistaGoHomestay @VisualElite @VisualMediaPro @visualnarrative
@visualphone @vitalityrocket @vitalnutrients @VitalOxide @vitaltweets @vitalyvt @Vitta360Global @VivaViaNomads @VivekavonRosen @vivianb53 @vivianltk
@VividEpiphany @VividMarketing @vivienneho @VivitaGirl @vivvos @vixwrld @viziondanz @VizzTone @VJLasorsa @VJVazquez @vknipper @VKovalenko
@vladikus999 @vladonpoker @vlddlv @vlemx @vmarketingguru @vmcmurray @VMPCC @vmsajan @vnetpulse @VOAGNO @vocetweets @Vodbay @voiceoftexas
@voilalalal @VoipComputer @VoipConference @VoIPStartsHere @volcom_sa @VolkerRupprecht @Vollkin @vollmerpr @VolntrMilwaukee @volodiakamenniy @voltrezman
@Volumeking @volvoshine @vonauff @VonGehrCG @vonkakus @VonReventlow @Voorsteegh @VOplanet_MS @vorigelevens @Voslin @Vote4Wallace @VoteGlobalPolls
@VoteMattSchultz @votenet @votescottaylor @VoxOptima @VProcunier @vpsean @VR4SmallBiz @vrdeals @vrental @VRIDETV @vrsocialmedia @vrwd @vscribe
@vsellis @vshimoyama @vshivone @vsNEWS @VSWoodPsyD @vtorresmx @VTravelTours @vtwit4u @vwinsuranceguru @VWworld @vyouz @VyralMarketing
@vyuh_in @VZWChandler @W_C_marketing @W_Debauchez @W_Rutledge @w0rdpress @w2e @w2Fund @w2scott @W2WIT @w3buck @waahootravel @waalston

@Wacoboard @wadebroder @wadever @wagandt @wagerking @wahagain @wahbi63 @wahgypsy @WahMagzine @wahoocandyman @wakeup2life @wakooz @Wakooz_RSS @Wakooz_RSSfeeds @waku_waku @walaaumedia @Waldo_Bar_None @waldowaldman @Wales_Online @walidmrealtor @WalkerTaft @WalkerWork @walkies1 @Walking1974 @walkscotland @wallglamour @WallopOnDemand @Wallpapers_Cool @WallStGems @wallstickersau @wallstpick @WallStreetGrand @walshcollege @walshypop2010 @walter_fischer @WalterAacf @WalterGordy @walterkb79 @WalterRose @waltonsearch @Wandafay @WanderingWilbo @wanderlustmktg @Wandia_Info @wantandblog @Wanting2Succeed @wanttogetfree @Warcraft_Guides @WarcraftMastery @WardBurksPD @warkmalsh @WarnerCarter @warosesr @warrencass @WarrenMason @WarrenPeas @WarrenTan @WarrenWhitlock @warriorlight @waspdesign @Wasteawaygroup @waterdesign @WaterwayRealty @WatkinsLadybeth @WattersCreek @WaveScript @WavesGratitude @waxing_lounge @waybackengine @Wayne_Belair @Wayne_D_Brown @Wayne_Faye @Wayne_Walker @wayne1120 @wayne1169 @wayne1hutchins @WayneBreitbarth @WayneHurlbert @WayneMansfield @WayneMarr @waynermb @waynevaughn @WayoftheWizard @wayrustic @WBaranowski @wbaustin @WBHBoston @wbidiwale @wbill1 @wbrnet @wbryuocc1684 @WCCOBreaking @wclements @WComGroup @wcs2 @wcweeks @wcwellness @WDCB @wdccdisney @WdenTonkelaar @wds7 @WDT_Schubert @WDYC @We_bestseller @weakwolves @wealth_builder7 @Wealth2050 @WealthBuilderNY @wealthbuilding @wealthbychoice @wealthcreation9 @WealthEvite @WealthForTeens @WealthForYou @wealthtoday @WealthyAfiliate @wealthysmurf326 @WealthyState @WeareNation1 @wearesocial @WeatherPlanet @WeaverContent @WeaversWay @web_host_info @web_news @web_preneurs @web_wacko @web2_smm @web20_marketing @web2client @Web2Greg @web2guru @web2rule @web2summit @Web4pointO @WebAdMetrics @WebAdvantage @webalicious @webanatics @WebBadgerBrock @webbizceo @webbizmarketing @WebBrainiac @webbrauser @WebBusinesses @WebBuyz @WebcastCity @WebConnect411 @webcurl @webdefenders @WebDesign_info @WebDesign6 @webdesignfan @webdesignleads @WebDesignPeoria @WebDivaAshley @WebDonuts @WebErika @webermedia @WebExperiment @webfaststart @WebForceOne @WebFugitive @webgabs @WebGeekPH @WebGossip @WebGridAds @webheadservice @WebHealthClinic @WebHealthMag @WebHost697 @webhostdir @webi5 @Webinetry @WebinetryJA @webinfomktg @webist @Webjutsu @weblaunches @WeBlogtheWorld @WebMallOnline @WebMarketing123 @webmarketingmav @WebMarktngCOACH @webmasterananya @webmasterfr @webmastergeek @webmastersc @webmastery @webmediaexpert @WebmetricsSpain @webmktinggroup @WebMktrsSpk @webnextstep @WebNoos @webomac @weboptimiser @weborglodge @WebPaz @webpos @webpresencewiz @webprofitz @WebPRpro @webrecruit @WebrecruitJobs @webresident @webs_craic @websatan @websavvymoms @WebScheduling @WebsElevators @websitedevel @websitegratuit @Websites4Result @websitesdotcom @websitessoft @websmith1 @websnacker @websocialmediaM @WebSolarStore @websolutions1 @WebStatements @WebStrategyShop @WebStudio13 @websuccessdiva @WebSuccessGurus @websuccessideas @webtechblog @webtickle @webtrafficnet @webtrepreneur @WebTVWire @webtweetwizard @WeBuyWithCash @webvideocoach @WebVideoMax @webws @Webzie @WECAI @WeCanDoItFRW @weddingflorist @weddingsbytracy @weddingz @WedgeLee @wedirectllc @wednesdayadams1 @weedott @weejeemedia @WeekDate @weeklyroast @weeklystandard @WeeklyWebinar @WeGayFriends @wehype @WeightCoach4U @WeightForAge @WeightLoss1st @WeightLoss86 @WeightLossFit @weightlosshelpr @weightlossking2 @WeightOffDude @weightprograms @WeightWatchers_ @weimin2008 @weiran_li @weirdchina @weirdchina2 @weirdnews @WeirdNewsForU @weirdralph @weissallison @WeiYoongLim @weknowmore @welintonlori @welittler @wellbeinglive @wellbelove @wellness_guide @wellness4all @wellnessbill @wellnessblast @wellnessexpo @WellnessNut @WellnessSpa24 @Wellsleypark @welltalkradio @WellWire @welovejbyeah_x @WeLoveSoaps @wenbryant @WendiMooreAgncy @Wendistry @wendroffcpa @wendy_moore @wendycwilliams @wendyflanagan @wendygelberg @wendymarx @WendyMaynard @WendyMLMSinger @Wendytaylor01 @wendyweiss @WeNetProfit @WenHud @wentzeldk @WeppoCom @WEPromote @weRaustin @werdemillionaer @weRhouston @Werkadoo @WernerKamphuis @Wesbo @weseebusiness @wesellnmail @wesjohnson8 @weskriesel @WesleyHendriks @westeross @WestHorse @westkirbysailin @westonwoodward @WestSoundTech @WestVil @Westwindsa @WetFeet_Career @wettgiggles @wewantitall @WeyLessNow @WezPyke @WFAAalexa @wfaaizzy @wfaashelly @wfmkt @WFP @WFTVShows @wgaultier @wgcommunities @wgooden @wgpasunny1100 @wh_education @wh_health @whackonly @Whale2020 @Whaleoil @WhatamanJackson @whatawebsite @whatchawearing @WhatIsOnNet @whatloversdo @whatma @WhatOdor @WhatsHappN @WhatsHappnRVA @WhatsHappnVA @whatshedoinnow @whatskochin @whatsthepoint_ @whattoknow @whatwecallarose @WHBsolutions @whchaminda @wheatgrassplace @wheelchairsteve @wheelchiro @wheelcipher @whentoyzattack @wheredallas @whereisannabel @whereivebeen @whereNewOrleans @whereRyou @WHHG_InMotion @whichforex @whichwich @WhichWichDFW @WhichWichHou @WhistlerGroup @WhistleTweets @whistlezzz @whitehatmedia @whitehausny @WhiteWallsArt @whitgorham @whitneypannell @WhitRecruiter @whitsundays @whoisjob @WhoIsWaterman @whojin @WholeFoods @WholeFoodsDFW @wholesaleautos1 @WholesaleJohn @wholesalemaster @wholesaler @wholeself @whomq @WhoopSays @whorunsgov @whosbackstage @whosChrisHughes @whosty @WhosYourAnnie @WhoYaWearin2day @whoyouhatin @WhyGeorge @WhyProperty @WhyReese @whySquidoo @whywetweet @Wi_FiMAN @wickedjava @WiderScreenings @wifeycha @wigoutnow @wigs_ @wigsuperstore @wii101 @wiifanatic @wikiHow @Wild_Chloe @wildcatloren @WildcatWire @wildeidea @wilderinbound @wildinspire @wildlifeaid @WildlySuccesful @WildMountain @WildPeekDesign @wildskye @WildwatersLodge @WildWebWomen @wildwestbob @WilElliott @wilhelser @wiliamki11 @will_ran @WillBerthiaume @willbobby @willemrt @WillEnglishIV @willfrancis @william_lee @williamarruda @WilliamAston @WilliamBforLess @WilliamBrant @WilliamCoquerel @williamEd1975 @WilliamLark @williamoo06 @WilliamRamirez6 @williamroe @williamscafeoak @williamscott1 @WilliamsKim @WilliamWomack @williebaronet @willierandle @williestylez @williger @WillisClark @willisteam @williwyss @WILLKUmy @willofnature @willowyspirit @WillPao @WillPaysTheBill @WillRogersUSA @willylim @WillyWonksUF @wilmallan @wilmer2004 @WilsonBooo @wilywenches @wimbeunderman @Win_Control @win_together @Win2012GOP @Windbaron @windlegends @windowshop_Mt @WindowsHowToDo @WindPowerSystem @WindsorHills4u @WindsorHillsClb @windycitysocial @Wine_Connection @WINE_DINE @wine594 @wineauctioneer @winedinners @WineDiverGirl @WineInside @WineMcGee @wineOmoms @wineportfolio @winerecipes @Winereview @WineSouthAfrica @winetrends @WineTwits @WineWithTheGuys @winnevents @Winning_MLM @winninghelix @winnitcouk @WinnWins @winsoar @winstontaylorUK @WintersOnline @winwithsue @wipplet @Wipro @WireACake @wiredmessenger @wiredmoms @wireless_phones @WirelessButler @wirjetzthier @wisdomalive @wisebread @WiseDreams @wisematize @Wisepreneur1 @WiseQuotes @Wisestepp @wisewomanwoods @Wish2Earn @wishes2u @wishnie @wishopen @witneybeverly @witqld @wits29usa @wittlake @wizardgold @wizardofwords @wizardssecret @WizardSurf @WizardUbiz @Wize_Print_AZ @wjaegel @wjasynthesis @WjyMPk @wlockhart @wlstreet @WLVideoMessages @WM_Recordings @wmcolesmith @wmdean @WmJHartman @WMMadv @wmwinc @wnabcreative @Wntz @woaikjkong @wolfepk1 @wolfie3556 @Wolfram2112 @WolfwoodXLV @womanbehappier @Womanifesting @Womanocracy @WomansDay @women_power @Women_Worldwide @Women4ChevyVolt @womenbizlisting @WomenGunOwners @WomeninCrimeInk @WomenProNetwork @womenrepublic @womensar @WomensCampaign @WomensLingerie @womensproducts @womentorz @womenwhowine @WominBiz @WOMWorldNokia @WonderfulCA @WonderNBeAmazed @Wonderwordy @WonderWy @WoNoJo @WoodenBearCabin @Woodenhawk @Woodfloorpro @woodkatm @Woodland_Ridge @woodlandslawyer @woodswine @woodworkingsite @woofcp @woofette30 @woohoo56 @wookiemunch @wordchick @WordFrame @WordFromWlSt @wordmartini @WordofChrist @wordondernemer @wordpress_on_ms @WordpressPlug @WordPressWizard @WordRock @Words101 @WordsBySusan @wordsdonewrite @wordsideas @WordStream @Wordstrumpet @wordwrangler @wordywoman @work8homesucces @workathomejoe @workathometips @WorkCoachCafe @WorkDayRadio @workfmhomeDiva @workforceremix @workforvacation @workfromhome4u @workhomexpert @WorkInColour @workingvirtuall @workinseo @worklawyer @workmind @workNOLA @works_from_home @WorkTubeCV @workwithdave @workwithorlando @WorkWithSusanna @workwithted @Workwomenonline @World_of_DMCs @worldatlasman @WorldBlicx @WorldBlotter @Worldclass52 @worldcrisisbook @worldcruiser09 @WORLDHOTELS @worldimart @WorldinMotion @WorldNewsNet @worldnibber @worldofmarble @WorldofTea @worldpokerforum @WorldProNews @WorldStuffer @WorldSymbols @WorldUtopia @worldwidescam @WormScoop @Worob @wouldee5150 @woutervannierop @wowawebdesign @WOWbroadcasting @woweeone @wowtvmobile @wp7dev @wpbc @wpdealshare @wphash @wpinasecond @wpinternational @wpramik @wpside @wpsmash @WPstaff @wrapmybar @wravon @wrecycleit @wreichard @wrestlingandy @wright1foru @wrightreverend1 @WRiskManager @Write_GetPaid @WriteAdvantage @writebuy @writefly @WriteNowOP @writer_sheri @writer2go @writeauthorart @WriterChanelle @WriterChick47 @WriteResearch @WritersBlog @WritersRelief @writingfriend @WritingonLife @writtenbeat @wrross1 @wrzscene @WS49Texan @WSBTalkRadio @WSE123 @wsidom @wsinetpower @wsionlinebiz @WSIWebScience @wswarm @WtLossDoctor @WTNonline @wtoppert @Wulffy @Wulfmansworld @Wuxflux @wvanderbloemen @wvierra @WVIW @wvrknight @wvtwinklestar @wwater @wwcasey @wwediting @WWMPC_CEO @wwrcoach @wwwabidin @wwwIMtoolbox @wwWomenNetwork @wwwPoet @wwwwinwithsueco @wyattbrand @wycombeweb @WypMom @wysebrasil @wyvernaxe @wzzm13 @X10Rommel @x11r5 @xanpearson @xaviermir @XavierNelson @xavmonty @xBeckkks @xbitbird @xbitech @XBox360Free @xboxfreepoints @XcelAccounting @xcheater @xcheyanx @xclusiveflyers @xebwilson @xeduarda @Xeesm @XenonAsh @xerrex3 @XerRexDgrey @XERXESSS @xFranco @xgineer @xiam007 @xiaojing_chen @ximenarojas @XkikaXfran @xkinetic @Xlead @xlnation @xlntcommunicate @xMakaveli85x @xMellyJayne @xmizanx87 @XO7Brainiac @xobni @Xocai1chocolate @xodpod @XOJAPAN @xowiipro @XowiiTopteam @XPACS_CEO_Scott @xpanse @xpatcost @xpownit @xpressabhi @Xpressomarketin @XpressURNess @xQmail @XRobinson @xscenemidgetx2 @xtofke @Xtreme_Bieber @xtrememarketer @xtremepicks_com @XuanYA @xurxovidal @XxEmOShOrTyXx @xxlpay123 @xxrhodamyrnaxx @xxxlingerie @ya2sabe @yabar @YabberDigital @Yabednik @yacht_renting @YachtsByAce @Yahoo_Careers @Yahoo_Fanz @yahuauctions @YahyaHenry @yalechk @Yalitze @YamahaCommAudio @YaminiBhatt @YanceyG @yancyscot @Yangutu @yanisa5 @yanivjonathan @YannickvdBos @YanRozovsky @yanuzzi @Yapparent @Yapparently @yapstream @yardbird1964 @yardlighting @YasirKhan @YasminAishah @yasminbendror @yasniMe @yasonmasde10 @Yasser_Vidal @yasshi2009 @yawarecords @YayForFollowing @yayokay @YazTay @ybillingslea @ycdwyl @ycika01 @ycng @YCTtx @yeahem @YearOfAffiliate @yellowdogPG @yellowsuits @YellowtailFP @YesItsOrganic @YESUmob @YesuRohi @yettamae @yewcom @yiannig @yidio @YIGALCOHEN @ykmrsw @Ylice @ylingz @yllib @YNHMedia @yoBarney @YODspica @YODspica_Best @Yoep_com @yoga_mama @yogaangel71 @YogaArmy @YogaBistro @yogaheals @YogaNewsNow @YogaUpdates @YohRach @yoitsadrian @yolishemp @yomecomunico @yominpostelnik @YORanchSteaks @yorel95 @yoshuadaely @yoTwentyOne @youarefiredboss @youarefoxy @YouAreMobile @youbring2 @YouEarn6Figures @youlsa @Young_and_Busty @youngandbrave @YoungAVONLady @youngjbrooks @YoungLatinoNtwk @youngmankang @youngmax4 @youngmel @YoungYouCorp @YouniqueBiz @younmetweet @younyh @your_loans @Your_Say @Your8tweeT @yourbadcredit @yourchapter11 @YourChessCoach @yourcrystalball @yourdailytask @YourDreamJob @YourEmployment @YourEzineCoach @YourFreeATM @yourgop @YourHeritage @YourHomeTeamAdv @yourjobmyoffice @YourLifeHappens @YourLittleAcre @yourLuxuryLANE2 @yourmentor08 @yournetbiz42 @YourPort @YourProfileNow @yoursalescopy @YourShoeStore @YourTechAdviser @YourtePrestige @YourVitaminLady @yourway2theweb @YourWebGuide @YourWebPresence @YourWillMatters @YourWritingDept @youthgrouptee @YouTractorCom @youtubeadvert @YoutubeGeeks @YoutubeHits @youtuberealest8 @Youvebeentagged @YoYoYear2010 @ypcPaul @YRSkudder @YRTMedia @ysabelvel @yslanrulz @YTeutsch @ytomei @yukisek @yumichen @yumiliciouscup @YUNG_RICK @yungLeezyy @yungmemphis @YuriAll @yurself @yusep_aja @yvettegr @Yvonneloveslife @YvonneLyon @YvonneWolo @yweic @YZZYpl @zaah @zablud @ZabreDVD @Zach_ary @ZacharyMeiu @ZacharySkinner @zachbow @zachhornsby @ZachSlobin @zack_miller @zackcovell @ZackLuby @zaellen @zaffi @ZagatWineClub @ZAGrrl @ZahidaKhan @zaibatsu @ZaibatsuPlanet @zaifmand @zakaraya @Zakta @Zalisrg @ZamTravel @ZamZuuShopping @zapalaFZK @zappatier @zarvo @zayuk @ZaZaDallas @ZaZaGallery @zazo @ZazZyu @zbeckman @zbellak @zbest_global @ZBizforSEO @zbizinc @zbleumoon @zBusinessCoach @zddesign @ze_machyne @ZE2Media @Zea_Restaurants @zeannjian @zebeauty @zebracross @zebrawear @zebrun @zebu75 @zecashtank @ZechParker @zedbiz @zeebat @zeepha @ZeeVisram @ZeezleEarth @zeiisgomess @Zeitarbeit_Info @zeitgeist69 @Zelia @zemarketing @zenaweist @zenbeats @zenbitch @ZenBizTools @ZenDoc @ZenfulDance @zenofjen @Zenonesearch @zenorocha @ZENSUSHI @ZenTechMaster @zepponi @zer0friction @zeroDOTin @ZeroNineRacing @ZeroToRiches @zerotosold @zeus8894 @zhabuk @zhengjingjing96 @ZhuZhuHamsters @Ziing_dot_com @zijamoringa @zijisdemakelaar @Zimmermitch @zimpeterw @zininweb @ZINplicity @Zipaah @ZipGiveSudbury @zippycart @ziptheusa @zirahnliz @ZnaTrainer @zoenewcombe @zoenfriends @ZoesDFW @zoeyshea @ZOMAGAZINE @ZombieRiot @ZombieStuff @zonabidesign @zonefraud @zonerdck @zonki @zonlyone @Zoom_1 @ZOOM7events @ZoomerangCJ @Zoomphed @zoomphotograph @zoomtechtv @zoomzio @zoozli @zoranewyork @ZOS84 @ZoyaBurda @zritter @zudhy @zulemagvg @zulkar004 @ZurvitaShelley @zutroi @ZvonkoPavic @Zwinkycharacter @zyakaira @zyonhosting @Zystal @zytechx @ZZ0 @zzcrawfish @zzpboekhouder @ZZPnetwerk @zzpwerk